Education for Citizenship and Discipleship

Education for Citizenship and Discipleship

EDITED BY

Mary C. Boys

The Pilgrim Press

NEW YORK

Scripture quotations, unless otherwise indicated, are from the Revised
Standard Version of the Bible, copyrighted 1946, 1952, © 1971, 1973 by
the Division of Christian Education of the National Council of the
Churches of Christ in the U.S.A., and are used by permission.

Library of Congress Cataloging-in-Publication Data

Education for citizenship and discipleship.

   Companion vol. to: Tensions between citizenship
and discipleship.
   1. Christianity and politics.   2. Christian life—
1960–   .   3. Christian education.   I. Boys, Mary C.
BR115.P7E38   1989   261.7   88–32098
ISBN 0–8298–0796–9

The Pilgrim Press, 132 West 31st Street, New York, N.Y. 10001

Contents

Foreword

A CENTER FOR CONGREGATIONAL EDUCATION was begun in 1982 at Christian Theological Seminary, Indianapolis, supported by funding from the Lilly Endowment. One of the Center's most important projects was the formation of a National Faculty Seminar (NFS). This interdisciplinary and ecumenical group of eleven scholars met over three years (1983–86) to probe the relationship between American church life and education. This book and its companion volume, *Tensions Between Citizenship and Discipleship: A Case Study,* resulted from the sessions of the Seminar.

A broad question, formulated by a steering committee (Mary C. Boys, Sara Little, C. Ellis Nelson, and Nelle G. Slater) prior to the initial session of the Seminar, inaugurated discussion: "How shall we interpret the Christian faith to educate for the future good of the world?" In the nine meetings that followed, the scholars engaged in a lively exchange across a range of issues and perspectives.

A concurrent project sponsored by the Center for Congregational Education was a postdoctoral year of study in Christian education. Scholars who already held a doctorate in a field of theological studies other than religious education engaged in a year of studies designed to strengthen their deepening interest in religious education. In addition, they participated in the NFS during their year of appointment.

Special gratitude should be given to Robert W. Lynn, Senior Vice President of the Lilly Endowment, who initially proposed a seminar; and to Thomas J. Liggett, then President of Christian Theological Seminary, who so graciously hosted the Seminar sessions.

Nelle G. Slater
Director
Center for Congregational Education
Christian Theological Seminary
Indianapolis

Contributors

THE MEMBERS OF THE NATIONAL FACULTY SEMINAR

DOROTHY C. BASS   Associate Professor of Church History,
Chicago Theological Seminary

MARY C. BOYS, S.N.J.M.   Associate Professor of Theology and
Religious Education, Boston College

DON S. BROWNING   Alexander Campbell Professor of Religion
and Psychological Studies, Divinity School, University of
Chicago

WALTER BRUEGGEMANN   Professor of Old Testament, Columbia
Theological Seminary

JOHN A. COLEMAN, S.J.   Professor of Religion and Society,
Jesuit School of Theology and The Graduate Theological
Union

BERNARD J. COOKE   Professor of Theology, Holy Cross College,
Worcester

THOMAS F. GREEN   Margaret O. Slocum Professor of Education
and Adjunct Professor of Philosophy, Syracuse University

KAREN LEBACQZ   Professor of Christian Ethics, Pacific School of
Religion

SARA P. LITTLE   Critz Professor of Christian Education, Union
Theological Seminary in Virginia

C. ELLIS NELSON   Visiting Professor of Christian Education,
Austin Presbyterian Theological Seminary

NELLE G. SLATER   Professor of Christian Education, Christian Theological Seminary

The postdoctoral scholars: Anthony Dunnavant, Edward Everding, Robert Goldstein, David Hester, Ronald Kernaghan, D. Cameron Murchison, Jr., Minka Sprague.

Introduction

THE RELATIONSHIP OF RELIGION TO POLITICS has been a perennially controversial topic. Today, however, in the light of ecclesial statements on nuclear war, church participation in actions of civil disobedience, and the high visibility of the so-called "Christian Right" on the political scene, there is a broader public awareness, coupled with wariness, about the entanglement of religious and political commitments.

The issues involved in untangling religion and politics are, of course, stubbornly resistant to any simple resolution; further, they are complicated by the particular way they take shape in a nation with a tradition of the separation of church and state.

While giving no list of solutions, this book provides a means of thoughtful entry into the topic by framing the discussion in terms of the dual responsibilities of citizenship and discipleship. Hence, this question is central: "How might we appropriately educate disciples who are responsible citizens?"

In fact, the essays in this book originated from a similar question posed to members of the National Faculty Seminar at their first gathering in 1983: "How shall we interpret the Christian faith to educate for the future good of the world?" This question, deliberately couched in the broadest terms, invited each scholar to participate in a common enterprise of rethinking the ways the church educates, drawing upon his or her own field for wisdom and insight.

Though no magic solutions surfaced, at least three significant results became apparent. The first was the educative nature of the seminar itself. The breadth of the question allowed participants to shape the particular direction they perceived. Moreover, there was an extraordinary dialogical character to the sessions—a tone that, regretfully, does not always characterize academic exchange. Each of the nine meetings was *zestful:* scholars listened thoughtfully to one another, asked probing questions, modified their views as new perspectives were offered, and entered wholeheartedly into their common project. As Sara Little points out in her concluding essay, not only did members of the Seminar think *about* education, they *were themselves educated* in the very process.

Second, the focus—*education for citizenship and discipleship*—which emerged midway through the three-year period of the Seminar offers a unique, interdisciplinary study of a vital topic. For all of the growing public awareness of the complicated relationship of religion to politics, little has appeared that explores in any depth the responsibilities of educators in the churches. More typically, publications have been programmatic in intent—curricula for social justice, for example; or topical—such as linking themes of liberation theology with particular educational strategies. The question underlying this volume is more fundamental.

Third, the essays in this book are closely tied to a companion volume, *Tensions Between Citizenship and Discipleship: A Case Study.* As members of the Seminar discussed issues around the underlying question, they decided to test it in the light of a specific case: a congregation's decision to grant sanctuary. Over the months, essays for both volumes were exchanged, discussed, and edited; the case study helped to clarify more theoretical points, and the focus on education for citizenship and discipleship gave direction to the analyses of the case.

The Contents of This Volume

There are six interdependent essays, preceded by an introduction and followed by a postscript. While each essay stands on its own, the volume nevertheless has a clear unity: the dimensions of Christian obligation to love God and neighbor. How does one educate Christians to be both disciples and citizens?

In Part One, "Disciples and Citizens: Two Perspectives," Walter Brueggemann and John Coleman establish the framework of the volume in their common argument that Christians must be "bilingual." That is, Christians must learn both the communal language of their own tradition and the public language of the secular realm. Or, to use Brueggemann's metaphor, Christians must engage in conversations both "behind the wall" and "on the wall," respectively. He, however, stresses the priority of learning the communal language—which he terms "sectarian," or the language "behind the wall"—whereas Coleman, while also assigning precedence to developing a distinctively Christian pedagogy of discipleship, gives more emphasis to what the pursuit of citizenship can offer Christian disciples. Their common conviction and differing points of emphasis provide a clear focal point.

Four subsequent essays take up the implications of the Brueggemann-Coleman arguments. In Part Two, "Fundamental Theological and Educational Views," Bernard Cooke and Mary C. Boys lay out considerations basic to constructing a pastoral response. Cooke delineates five understandings fundamental to Christian self-understanding. He focuses on concepts every Christian must grasp in order to be both a disciple and a Christian. Cooke's essay might be viewed precisely as the conceptual undergirding of Brueggemann's thesis: what one needs to know in order to be Christian. Boys situates the discussion of citizenship and discipleship in the context of the field of religious education—a specialization that few theologians understand. She provides a map of the field and then locates the discussion about educating for citizenship and discipleship.

Don Browning and Karen Lebacqz, in Part Three on "Implications for Theological Education," ask questions proper to their disciplines of pastoral care and ethics, respectively. Browning argues at the methodological level, situating the discussion of citizenship and discipleship in the context of his understanding of "practical theology." And since practical theology as he understands it is based on a revised correlational model, it is pluralistic and public—a view that indicates Browning's advocacy of Coleman's point of view more than Brueggemann's. Browning proposes that equal regard for the neighbor lies at the heart of a normative civil ethic guiding citizenship; to this, Christian discipleship adds a narrative and visional structure, particularly concerning the necessity of self-sacrifice. Lebacqz focuses on the processes of educating for justice, with a particular eye toward pain as a resource for education. Hers is a creative development of Brueggemann's point about the necessity of the sectarian community's need to make pain "an inescapable public reality by bringing it to speech." Lebacqz argues that critical rationality does not suffice for an adequate grounding in ethics and that painful confrontation may well be a necessary pedagogical tool for conversion to the life of the disciple.

In a final essay, a "postscript," Sara Little traces common themes in the essays, relating them to the question that initiated the seminar. Her essay is particularly useful both for explicating the interdependence of the essays and for gaining a sense of the dialogue so important to the composition of this volume.

Thus, from start to finish, the essays are oriented toward the educational work of the church in the formation of disciples and citizens.

I am grateful to all of the members of the National Faculty Seminar for their commitment to our work. I owe a particular debt to Nelle Slater, director of the Center for Congregational Education at Christian Theological Seminary and editor of the companion volume: her wise administration has been key to the Seminar. In addition, I wish to acknowledge each of those members whose essays are included herein; their prompt response to deadlines greatly facilitated the editing process. Thanks are due to Maureen O'Brien, a doctoral student at Boston College, who has been immensely helpful to me in every phase of this project.

MARY C. BOYS
Boston College

PART I

Disciples and Citizens: Two Perspectives

1

The Legitimacy of a Sectarian Hermeneutic: 2 Kings 18—19

Walter Brueggemann

A BEGINNING POINT for our study may be found in the dramatic encounter between the Assyrians and Judah in 2 Kings 18:17–27 (cf. Isaiah 36:11–12). Conventionally the event is dated 701 B.C.E. The Assyrian army is at the gate of Jerusalem, ready to negotiate, or rather to receive a surrender. The city is under siege. The context is a gross mismatch between imperial power and a tiny kingdom without visible resources. Assyria has sent its negotiating team in the person of the Rabshakeh. The Assyrian strategy is to evoke a surrender so that a forceful invasion is not necessary.

The drama takes place in two parts, which will suggest a way to state our problematic.

1. *The conversation at the wall of the city.* The Assyrian negotiator stands at the city wall and shouts the terms of surrender. In part he makes an offer (18:31–32). But mostly he taunts. He argues that Judah has no real alternative to surrender. Certainly trust in YHWH is not an alternative, for the negotiator's imperial reason convincingly makes clear that this is a false reliance. He likens YHWH to all the other pseudo-gods of the Near East who have failed, and he understands that this one also will fail.

The response of the agents of King Hezekiah to this public form of negotiation is this: "Speak to us in Aramaic. Do not speak to us in the language of Judah [i.e., Hebrew] in the hearing of the people." That is, speak to us in the language of international diplomacy. Speak to us in the language of sophisticated, public imperial negotiation which the common folk do not understand. Because if you speak Hebrew, they will understand, and we cannot have confidential negotiations. The common people will hear what you say. And you will persuade them, because they will be terrified. In this response, the Assyrian negotiator understands the point well. He deliberately answers "in the language of Judah" (v. 28). That is, he goes over the heads of the leadership and engages in an act of intimidation which makes negotiation impossible.

2. *There is also a conversation behind the wall.* Here the Judeans speak only to one another. Here Hebrew is spoken, not Aramaic, for the folks there do not all understand Aramaic. Back of the wall, inside the city, a different language is spoken by a different set of people with a different agenda. The leadership is baffled by what went on at the wall. And upon instruction from the king, they did not answer the Assyrians directly (18:36).

Then behind the wall, out of sight of the Assyrians, the king does grief work. He goes to the house of the Lord (19:1). The leadership summons the prophet Isaiah to pray for the king and for the city. The invitation is based in the fact that Assyria has *mocked* YHWH. And YHWH will surely rebuke and repudiate such a mocking. The conversation behind the wall (unlike the conversation on the wall) does not doubt the power of YHWH, even against the power of the empire. The very God whom the Assyrians liken to the other gods is here singled out as "the living God" (19:4), utterly unlike the other gods.

The response of Isaiah is in 19:6–7: "Do not be afraid [of the empire]." It is the word of YHWH. It is a remarkable word, surely a word that would not have credibility on the wall. It is a terse word, and it is followed by more Assyrian taunting (19:8–13), a prayer about mocking by Hezekiah (19:15–20), an oracle of response from Isaiah (19:21–28), and a narrative reporting that the city was saved (19:35–37). The actual report of deliverance at the end of the narrative is linked to the initial oracle of Isaiah in

19:6–7. The saving of the city vindicates the prophet, relieves the king, and asserts that YHWH is more powerful than the imperial threat. That is, the characterization of YHWH behind the wall as the living God is in fact more discerning than the conversation at the wall which dismissed YHWH by analogy with other failed gods. It is dramatically important that these two conversations go on at the same time. The Assyrians on the wall have no access to the conversation behind the wall. They do not know it is going on. And if they did, they would not believe it. But it turns out to be decisive for relating to the empire. The empire in this situation is impinged upon decisively by the conversation behind the wall.

I

As we move from this text, three qualifications are in order:

1. The critical problems of this text and its parallel in Isaiah 36—37 are acute, as outlined by Brevard Childs.[1] I do not presume that this is flat historical reporting, but it is simply a text that proposes a reading of reality. That much can be discerned in the text without sorting out all the historical difficulties.

2. You will understand that I do not read the text in terms of simplistic fideism, as though prayers to God are a direct way in which to refute the empire. The hermeneutical issues are much more complicated, though I do not wish simply to abandon the faith claim asserted here any more than I wish to affirm it simplistically.[2] But I take the text as one mapping of our question of sectarian hermeneutics.

3. Obviously in moving from this text, I have chosen a certain model for our discussion. Other texts could have been chosen offering other models. It may seem to you that this is not a helpful model because it maps the exchange of public discourse and sectarian discourse as conflictual. I pursue it this way because I hope it illuminates the subject assigned to me and because I believe it is illuminating for the context of church education in American society. To be sure, other texts and models might have been chosen that offer a happier interface between the two conversations.

In any case, in this text as model I suggest that people of faith in public life must be *bilingual*. They must have a *public language* for negotiation at the wall. And they must have a more *communal language* for processing behind the gate, in the community, out of sight and range of the imperial negotiators. Such a view may seem harsh on the imperial negotiators as a type. Perhaps they are not always so hostile and perhaps more common ground can be found. But the truth of the matter is that they speak a different language which for the community behind the wall is not only a foreign language but a secondary language in which serious matters are not primally expressed.

In this text, Aramaic is public language. And when that language is spoken, this believing community has no privilege or advantage. On the other hand, Hebrew is here community language. It is the language in which members of this community of commitment speak to one another. The different language (Hebrew) permits a different conversation. Now the talk is to YHWH (in prayer) and about YHWH. In this language which would be silly in the presence of Assyria, YHWH is reckoned as a live force, as a real character in dramatic reality. Indeed in Hezekiah's prayer, YHWH is referred to as "the living God," the God who has power to make a difference (19:6, as in 19:4). And the conversation is carried on by different characters, especially Isaiah, who never appears on the wall, who never, as far as we know, speaks Aramaic, but who confines himself to conversation behind the wall. That is remarkable, because Isaiah is commonly regarded as the most urbane and cosmopolitan of all the prophets. But even he stays behind the wall in this sectarian conversation. And the outcome of this conversation behind the wall, as the story has it, is the decisive conversation, not the one on the wall.

My urging is that church education must be bilingual, nurturing people to know the language to speak on the wall in the presence of the imperial negotiators and to speak the language behind the wall in a community of faith where a different set of assumptions, a different perception of the world, a different epistemology are at work. The conversation on the wall is crucial, because the Assyrians are real. They are dialogue partners who must be taken seriously. And they will not go away. But unless there is another conversation behind the wall in another language about another agenda, Judah on the wall will simply submit to and echo imperial perceptions of reality. And when imperial perceptions of reality prevail, then everything is already conceded. If the conversation with the empire at the wall is the only conversation or the decisive one, then Israel will decide that YHWH is indeed like all the other important gods and consequently will endorse imperial policies as nonnegotiable realities. For the ground for any alternative will have been forfeited.

It is interesting that in 18:27 the Assyrian negotiators seem to have no respect for the speakers of Hebrew: "Has my master sent me to speak these words to your master and to you, and not to the men sitting on the wall, who are doomed with you to eat their own dung and to drink their own urine?" And so in v. 28, the Rabshakeh addresses them in their own language. But in v. 36, they do not answer. I suggest they refuse to answer the Assyrians' Hebrew and to accede to Assyrian perceptions of reality because they understood that his Hebrew was fake Hebrew, spoken with an odd accent by one who did not know the nuance of the language or the nuances of the conversation behind the wall. The language *behind* the wall is dysfunctional *on* the wall. Those who speak the language behind the wall when on the wall are likely to be irrelevant. And an attempt to use it there misunderstands and betrays the power and claims of that alternative language which is not to include the outsiders.

An argument needs to be made about both languages. But because of my assigned topic, I will speak only of the second language, the one behind the wall, the *language of sectarian hermeneutic*.

II

With this narrative encounter as the focus of our study, we must pause to consider the elements of our assigned topic. The terms are heavily freighted and not unambiguous.

1. *Hermeneutic.* The term "hermeneutic" requires us to acknowledge the depth of ambiguity and relativity in every process of reading reality. There is no obvious, clear, or unambiguous reading of reality. Neither the conversation on the

wall nor the conversation behind the wall can claim to be simply descriptive. Both conversations construct reality as much as receive reality. Both conversations are imaginative and work from a vested interest. That much is acknowledged in our title. And that in itself is important to church education. Put simply, interpretation theory[3] is the lens, the perspective, the bias through which experience is processed.

In our narrative, interpretation was going on at the wall (in public language). And it was going on behind the wall (in communal language). Quite clearly there are very different interpretative situations. Not only the language is different but the subject matter and the participants are different. On the wall the empire does the speaking. The agenda is the imperial system. That system has nullified every other truth claim. In this conversation no prophet speaks, for a prophet is by definition excluded from imperial talk. Also excluded along with the prophet is YHWH. Behind the wall, the agenda is the delivering God of the exodus who is a decisive figure in the drama, and the prophet does the decisive interpreting. No imperial voice is sounded here.

The two conversations scarcely overlap. But they are about the same reality. The issue hinges on which is the true conversation. Is it true that a serious agenda must include prophet and the living God because they really matter? Or is it true that these are imagined characters in a play that has no contact with reality? What constitutes social reality? Without deciding which is the true conversation, the text knows only that there are two conversations going on, and Israel must participate in both interpretative enterprises. Israel, like us, does not want to choose between the two conversations, and perhaps cannot. The claim of the narrative as we have it, of course, is:

a. The conversation behind the wall makes a difference in what one says on the wall.

b. The conversation behind the wall has a prior claim. It permits one to be suspicious of the conversation on the wall and, indeed, to have some freedom in that conversation, even though the reality of Assyrian power is not nullified or disregarded. But the absolute claims of the empire are handled without intimidated naiveté, a fact made possible by other conversation.

2. *Sectarian.* The term "sectarian" conjures up for us narrowness and provincialism. Following the governing definitions of Ernst Troeltsch[4] (and derivatively, H. Richard Niebuhr[5]), a sect is a community that does not share in or participate in the commonly accepted definitions of reality. It operates out of a different practice of perception, epistemology, and language. It holds to a set of alternative values that it regards as the truth. That is, it seeks to construct for its members an alternative life-world.[6]

Out of that way of using the word, three comments seem important:

a. The breakdown of Western scientific globalism may invite us to take this very definition of sect, generally scorned by liberals, and see its positive role. The recovery of ethnic rootage (as in Alex Haley, and less happily in Michael Novak) and the recovering of special histories of pain (as in various liberation movements)[7] may help us see that an alternative perception of reality is not simply a defensive measure but may be an act of identity, energy, and power. Moreover, such specificity, we are learning in painful ways, exercises an important critical function to show that the large claims of the dominant reality cannot be taken at face value.

b. The danger in sect truth is not its claim per se. The danger is that the "truthing community" regards itself as having a monopoly on truth. And for the sect, truth must be kept from the larger community in order to keep it pure. Such a defensiveness reflects, not a concern for truth, but a concern for control and a fear that by submitting the claim to larger scrutiny the sect truth will not hold.

But sect truth as alternative need not be a protected, monopolized claim. It can be a proposal to the larger community,[8] a proposal of an interpretation (a reading of reality) in which the larger community can share and which will bear the scrutiny of the larger community. So in our text, Israel's particular discernment of truth is made available to the empire, even though that truth implies an assault on the dominant, imperial truth. The sect does not accommodate its truth. But on the other hand, it need not monopolize its sense of truth. It may share it in unaccommodating ways, knowing that such an alternative truth inevitably makes a bite against dominant truth. It may be a very important discernment not available to the dominant truth.

c. Obviously, I am not interested in making a formal, general case for sect truth. I mean only to attend to the action of Israel and its reading of reality. No doubt there are sect truths that exploit and abuse. So we must move from the formal to the substantive claims of Israel. The substantive claim of Israel's truth is that YHWH, the God of the exodus, is the living God (19:4, 16).[9] It is not argued that this living God is alive only in Israel, only behind the wall, only for Israel. It is a large claim intended to impinge upon public, even imperial perceptions of reality. The claim flows from Israel's special history of pain and rescue, which dares to say that the power toward life, justice, and righteousness will override every power of domination. That I take as a "sectarian interpretation." But it is an interpretation in which the empire is invited to participate, albeit at dear cost.

Thus far, concerning these terms, "sectarian hermeneutic" then, I mean the conversation behind the wall conducted in the language of the community, in which the prophet participates crucially, rooted in the memory of this community which intends to create a different discussion on the wall. The purpose of a sectarian reading of reality is in order to transform the conversation with the empire on the wall.

3. *Legitimacy.* The difficult term in our title is "legitimacy." One can take "legitimacy" in a commonsense way as: "Does it hold water." And that may be adequate. However, a more critical understanding of legitimacy is available in the work of Jürgen Habermas.[10] It is perilous to use his categories, first, because they are exceedingly difficult and convoluted, and second, because using them with a premodern text may be an objectional anachronism. But I shall try.

Habermas characterizes the crisis of legitimacy as the separation of instrumental functions of administration from expressive symbols that evoke assent.[11] By instrumental functions he means the autonomous, secularized, scientific modes of managing people, managing the means of production, and managing the supportive ideology. The crisis is that such administrative claims rest, he suggests, on appeals to power, deception, and pragmatism, because they are largely cut off from the symbols that genuinely authorize. And so one must cover over the loss of energizing symbols by more consumer goods, by diversionary activity, or by fabrication of false symbols.[12] Such a way is illegitimate because it does not touch the actual life of people. While the deception may prevail, it cannot be compelling at bottom and therefore is illegitimate.[13]

In the discussion at the wall, one may wonder about the imperial presentation of reality, the royal hermeneutic. Is it legitimate in the sense that Assyrian military and political claims cohere with the expressive symbols? As it is presented in the text, I think not. In 18:31–32, the illegitimacy of the imperial claim is evident. The speaker knows enough of Israel's root dream of "vine and fig tree" to use the code words. These words are surely words of primal legitimacy, because they encompass the most passionate yearning of Israel. They may be the Israelite equivalent of "peace and prosperity" that must be mouthed by every political leader in our situation. But then the imperial mode nullifies that dream, shows that the dream is not really understood, by offering a substitute vine and fig tree in another part of the empire. The assumption of the speaker is that one land is as good as another and seeing one vine and fig tree is seeing them all. Such a predictable instrumental reading of reality is utterly alien to the expressive symbol of Israel.[14] The empire seeks to *use* the expressive symbol which shapes Israel's imagination but misunderstands it and so employs it in ways of illegitimacy. And certainly the people who spoke Hebrew did not fail to discern the doublespeak. This imperial use violates Israel's central passion. The violation is probably not calculated or even recognized. It is simply the way empires proceed. And every Israelite who hears the offer knows immediately that the imperial proposal is a fraud, because it does not cohere with the root symbol.

But what about the counterproposal and its legitimacy? What of the discussion behind the wall? Does the sectarian reading of reality hold together the reality of experience, the necessary functions of administration and the expressive symbols that claim assent and generate energy?

My answer is twofold. Insofar as the conversation behind the wall holds to its primal language and its generative reference, it is indeed legitimate. Israel's conversation goes deep into its own peculiar experience, where it has found energizing symbols. This is articulated in Isaiah's word in 19:6 with the primal speech, "Do not be afraid";[15] in the sureness of Hezekiah that YHWH is a living God not to be mocked (19:6); and in the prophetic response of YHWH's self-assertion against the mocker (19:22–24). All of this speech (*a*) stays very close to the primal language of Israel, (*b*) focuses singularly on the reality of God, and (*c*) refrains from policy formation which is not the function of sectarian interpretation. So far so good.

But the conversation behind the wall departs from the legitimacy we have expected when it enters into policy formation that ignores primal language, shifts focus from God to the Jerusalem establishment, and makes a concrete political claim. In 19:32–34, the Jerusalem ideology seems to me to usurp functions from the proper conversation. In that claim, I suggest, the text makes sounds that are as self-serving as those of Assyria. And then the conversation behind the wall becomes another conversation like the one on the wall. Then it is no longer legitimate, because it is not a proposal that can be offered and received in public discourse. It is now self-serving and must be rejected. In contrasting the assertions of 19:1, 6, and 22–24 with 19:32–34, I make a distinction that I trust is faithful to the Protestant principle. A sectarian interpretation is valid so long as it clings to the singular holiness of God. But when the singular holiness of God is assigned to historical structures, it has become self-serving ideology.

So our definition of terms yields this much:

1. *Hermeneutic:* A proposal for reading reality through a certain lens. In this narrative, only two such lenses are available, that of the empire on the wall and that of Israel behind the wall.

2. *Sectarian:* An alternative offer of a reading of reality processed through the experiential lens of a particular community informed by its history of pain and hope.

3. *Legitimate:* A reading of reality that holds together human experience energizing expressive symbols and necessary administrative function.

The purpose of such sectarian interpretation as offered in our narrative is to authorize those who join the public conversation on the wall to be present freely, imaginatively, and critically. It is my impression that, had there been no conversation behind the wall, the conversation at the wall would have been preempted by an Assyrian reading of reality that appeared to be absolute, accounted for all the recognized evidence, and faced no serious criticism.

My provisional linkage to church education is this: church education is properly and legitimately sectarian if it nurtures an alternative reading of reality that can interface the dominant reading of reality freely, imaginatively, and critically. And if that "other conversation" is not under way, then the dominant reading of reality (which in our time I would characterize as "consumer militarism") will have its unfettered, uncriticized way. I have observed that the dominant rationality of the empire must be criticized because its power actions are separated from the truth of human suffering and human hope and are therefore illegitimate. I have observed that sectarian rationality must also be critiqued when it falls into the same trap, as indeed much sectarian conversation does. But a sectarian conversation kept open to its own language, its own experience, and its own proper reference is not only legitimate but essential to serious public discourse. Without the conversation behind the wall, the conversation on the wall will surely become a totalitarian monologue. Such a monologue does not notice pain and in its absoluteness is incapable of serious hope.

III

I do not believe that the Bible serves very often or very well directly for participation in the public discourse at the wall. That is not its intent, purpose, or character.[16] Rather, it intentionally nurtures the conversation behind the wall that is an urgent contribution to the public conversation at the wall. Largely, it is the case that the biblical conversation is in the dialect of the community, only rarely in the common language of the empire. That does not make it any less relevant or urgent but relevant and urgent only in a certain kind of way.

I want now to pursue some of the elements of this "conversation behind the wall," which become the Bible's offer to the public conversation.

First, the story of Israel *originates as a counterperception* of reality.[17] If one agrees that it is the Moses narratives (rather than the Genesis narratives) which are decisive for Israel's reading of reality, then the "counter" thrust of the text is, I think, unarguable. The text itself seems to presume this, because the pervasive metaphors and allusions are those of exodus-wilderness-land. And the social analysis of Norman Gottwald supports this in massive ways.[18] The primal narrative assertion of Israel's faith is that of an oppressed people yearning for and receiving emancipation from an oppressor empire. This is the historical claim of the text. This is the liturgic reenactment of the Passover.[19] This is the intention of Israel's education to its next generation (cf. Deuteronomy 6:4–10, 20–24).[20]

The foundational word that Israel entrusts to its young, the interpretative bias about which Israel cares most, is a critical analysis of dominant social reality as inhumane and to be rejected. The pivot of this offer of a life-world is that *"the Egyptians treated us harshly."*[21] That foundation of social analysis sets the main elements for time to come for the conversation behind the wall. The Egyptians always hope the harsh treatment will not be noticed or felt or brought to public expression. Or they hope it will be accepted docilely as necessary to affairs of state. But the sectarian hermeneutic of Israel tends to notice and to bring it to speech. The "sacred discontent" of Israel derives from this beginning point of pain brought to speech.

On the one hand, the exodus story is initiated and powered "from below," from the articulation and public processing of pain. *We cried out* (Exodus 2:23–25). That is the second aspect of the creedal formulation. Note well, it does not say simply that we hurt, but we found voice. The voice is a harsh, hostile, subversive voice filled with revolutionary hutzpah. We are not told how or why there was energy and courage for the cry. Perhaps it simply belongs to this odd people that it is a people that does not lose its voice. And not losing its voice, it never accepts the word of the empire as an absolute voice, because it always knows about another voice that is incongruous with the sure, unhesitating voice of the empire.[22]

Conformity, docility, subservience, and depression are not served by this story. The empire—Egyptian or Assyrian—does not mind oppressed people being hurt, so long as there is no public outcry. But there is here. Indeed this is what Israel's sectarian conversation is about, a cry of pain that destabilizes, assaults, and delegitimates every absolute imperial claim. Israel insists that the voice of pain brought to public speech is a decisive social reality always to be taken seriously. And that is the tradition in which the sackcloth of Hezekiah stands in 2 Kings 19:1ff.

I find it remarkable that we come so far in this sectarian conversation without reference to God. While I tremble about the implications of that fact, the first topic in this sectarian conversation is critique of dominant reason ("The Egyptians treated us harshly"). Then, and not before, it is affirmed that the critique and the voice of pain reach and mobilize God. God the liberator is not contained by the dominant reason and therefore can be impinged upon from underneath. But not by way of docility, only by way of harsh and impatient, irreverent assault. This sectarian conversation with God perhaps models and gives warrant for the conversation with the empire that is subsequently undertaken. But unless there is the permit of experience of pain and hope in the community, the public conversation will never happen. Thus the very factors of pain and hope which may be the ingredients of the sectarian community are increasingly unacceptable to the dominant rationality.

The second spin-off from the critical analysis of the dominant social reality is constructive. It is the covenant, the emergence of the metaphor "kingdom of God,"[23] and the derivative Torah as an alternative social practice. To be sure, there are more critical questions connected with covenant as social theory and religious construct than we can undertake. But with Martin Buber (before G. E. Mendenhall),[24] it is clear that the covenant and its Torah are not only a religious meeting and relationship; covenant and Torah are a serious proposal for an alternative way to organize social power. Gottwald has shown how the Torah may be understood as a social experiment of an egalitarian kind. Many examples may be drawn from Deuteronomy. We can refer to the decisive proposal of the year of Jubilee. And Paul

Hanson[25] has demonstrated this fact in the early laws of Exodus 21—23 which seek to reorganize social life in ways that break with the conventions of exploitation and domination. In each case the new social proposal is closely linked to the concrete memory of pain and emancipation. But what I most want to stress is that the Torah, while it no doubt borrowed from a common legal tradition in the Near East, is framed essentially in a sectarian conversation of Israel as an alternative to imperial reality. One can argue that the Torah of Israel is a proposal and offer made to the nations. But that is not its first function. Its first function is to provide a basis for organizing this community in an alternative way that distances social practice from the ways of the dominant rationality.

Only in its earliest period could Israel hope to form a social organization of its own. And that only for a brief time in a limited area.[26] But what the prophets indicate, and indeed the entire tradition, is that Israel continued to draw its main impetus from this sectarian conversation, even as it participated in, and contributed to, public discourse. Israel, of course, knew that social organization must reckon with Assyria. Hezekiah knew that. Isaiah knew that. But persistently Israel met Assyria with some counteroffers generated by its own sectarian conversation. Israel persistently moves against the dominant rationality, refusing to accept its definitions and values, refusing to be assimilated into this consciousness. I would identify the following three elements as decisive for Israel's sectarian reading of reality which it offers to the nations:

- A suspicion of all dominant definitions of reality, because they embody a harshness.
- A readiness to make pain an inescapable public reality by bringing it to speech.
- An imaginative proposal for ordering society in an alternative way.

It appears, by the terms proposed, that such an offer is legitimate, because it stays close to experience, it bespeaks energizing symbols, and it acknowledges administrative necessity. The conversation behind the wall is most vulnerable to criticism on this last point. It may be suggested that this conversation is never "realistic" about power realities. And from the point of view of Assyria or Egypt, it appears so. But in the provisions of Deuteronomy where the administrative elements are clearest, one can conclude that administration is accounted for, albeit in ways alien to the empire.[27]

The focus of all three elements, of course, is YHWH, the one regarded as "living" by those behind the wall and regarded as *impotent* by the empire at the wall. To be sure, the judgment "impotent" is a male metaphor. That is precisely the kind of verdict that an empire would render. It is the claim of YHWH that makes the counterproposal so problematic for the empire. It is problematic because YHWH does not appear to be such a force and because if YHWH is such a force, YHWH is a force not conducive to systemic management. So Israel must go to the public conversation without insisting on being the key actor in its own story. Israel must make its case at the wall in other language. But the sectarian conversation is all about YHWH, who becomes the invisible but powerful legitimator of this counterproposal in public discourse. Faithful Israel is never so taken in by the dominant consciousness that it forgets who it is who gives the courage and authority to counter official truth.

IV

Israel's sectarian conversation functions especially as a *critical* agent in the public conversation. That is, this narrative of *critique/ cry/alternative* keeps Israel from ever accepting the dominant consciousness as absolute. Israel's elemental suspicion regularly notices that what appears to be rational is in fact *interested* and that what appears to be objective is in fact *self-serving*. The empire wants it to appear rational and objective. It is the critical presence of YHWH that enables Israel to notice the reality of interest and self-service. Israel's alternative memory notices that what passes for public discourse is in fact a new sectarian proposal of an ideological kind.

In its heady season of origin, the sectarian narrative enterprise which is Israel had no failure of nerve. But there are evidences throughout history that when Israel had to exist in the presence of worldviews and rationalities that seemed successful and comprehensive, its own narrative enterprise was inadequate and an embarrassment. At the beginning of the monarchal period, there is evidence, in 1 Samuel 8:5, 20, of a yearning to be "like all the nations," even if it means the abandonment of its notion of YHWH as king. And at the end of the Old Testament period, the clearest example I know of such inadequacy and embarrassment occurs when the Maccabean generation, chagrined at circumcision in the Greek gymnasium, devised surgery to remove every sign of having been circumcised (1 Maccabees 1:15). Israel repeatedly experienced the conversation partner at the wall as having a hermeneutic, a rationality, a way of experiencing the world which seemed more fully adequate. And, of course, the persistent problem of a sectarian community is the seduction of the dominant culture.

It is the insistent conversation behind the wall that asserts that the conversation partner at the wall is seductive, does not have the final hermeneutic, should not be taken at face value, but is in fact only acting in a narrow self-interest under the guise of a general, common interest. In our text of reference (2 Kings 18— 19), for example, the Assyrian negotiators at the wall are not offering a policy in the general interest but under such a guise are pursuing Assyrian policy at the expense of all those behind the wall. And when the dominant conversation partner acts and speaks only from a narrow interest, that is sectarian. We are not accustomed to thinking of the voice of the empire as a sectarian voice. But so it is when it serves only a narrow interest. *Empire as sect* is a theme worth pursuing in our own situation, because it may be suggested that the voice of American power, for example, claims to be the voice of general well-being and may in a number of cases be only the voice of a narrow range of economic and political interests. The ideological guise is effective if large numbers of people can be kept from noticing the narrow base of real interest. That narrow base will not be noticed unless there is another conversation behind the wall that gives critical distance and standing ground for an alternative assessment. In ancient Israel, the prophets are the ones who regularly expose the voice of the empire as a sectarian voice not to be heard as a comprehensive, disinterested voice. The prophetic critique against the rationality of the empire is consistent:

- In Isaiah 10:5ff., Sennacherib is no doubt an instrument of YHWH. But he oversteps and imagines that his own strength and wisdom have accomplished his works (cf. Isaiah 10:13–14).
- Consistently in Jeremiah, Nebuchadnezzar and the Babylonians are agents of YHWH (cf. Jeremiah 25:9; 26:6), but by Isaiah 47, mistress Babylon is condemned for having acted not as means but as end.
- For Ezekiel, first Tyre (Ezekiel 28:2) and then Egypt (29:3, 9) make statements of autonomy, and so are sure to be destroyed.
- In Ezekiel 38—39, the enigmatic reference to Gog and Magog concerns the same overreading of the permit given by YHWH.
- In Daniel 4:33, Nebuchadnezzar becomes like an ox eating grass, because he has not properly deferred to the rule of YHWH.

Admittedly, I have cited the most extreme cases. But my subject requires such a stress. This way of presenting the public process of imperial history functions as a massive critique of an imperial reading of reality. It is critiqued because it is autonomous, that is, it is not addressed to the governance of YHWH. That could perhaps be only a quarrel between ideologies and an argument about which name is to be used for God. But the insistence behind the wall is that in the imperial rationality, there is an absence of restraint and limitation proper to creatures of YHWH. There is unbridled aggression and self-serving, a lack of humanness and compassion. The argument concerns not religious phrasing but social policy as well. It is the critique made by this sectarian perspective that the rationality of the empire lacks social vision which must be practiced by any power congruent with YHWH. This critique is characteristically not made in *principle*, but with reference to specific situations.

Such a critique (a dismissal in extreme cases of the imperial conversation partner at the wall) might lead to a retreat in the community that makes the critique. Such a judgment has the capability, if not the probability, of a kind of isolationism and particularism that not only critiques the voice at the wall but pretends there is no such voice and imagines that the only serious conversation is the one in the sectarian language behind the wall. Then the sectarian tradition itself becomes idolatrous and in turn must be critiqued. The most remarkable thing about this tradition of "sacred discontent" is that it contains within itself the sources from which to mount a critique of its own practice. An honest conversation behind the wall critiques the empire when it becomes sectarian. It can also be self-critical concerning the temptation of the sect to make too much of itself.

So this particular sectarian hermeneutic (not every sectarian hermeneutic) contains the capacity to critique its own sectarianism. I mention five such critiques made from within the tradition, though others could be cited.

1. The *YHWHist tradition* on the Pentateuch would seem to be a major international move when the election tradition of Israel is freshly articulated with reference to a new internationalism.

a. Hans Walter Wolff[28] has seen that the programmatic formula is, "By you all the families of the earth shall bless themselves" (Genesis 12:3; 18:18; 22:18; 26:4; 28:14). That is, by a theology of blessing, it is argued that Israel's well-being is somehow linked to that of other nations. There is no blessing that can be monopolized without reference to the others. Put in programmatic fashion, Israel exists in the world for the sake of the nations, as a means and not as an end. Or put another way, the conversation behind the wall is for the sake of the partners at the wall. While it may come from elsewhere, one evidence of this line of argument is apparent in Jeremiah (of all places) in his well-known promise threat: In the welfare of the city will be your welfare (Jeremiah 29:7). That is, the future well-being of Israel is intimately linked with the well-being of Babylon.

b. Though the critical problems are difficult, it is plausible that some form of the Joseph narrative belongs in the world of the YHWHist. Von Rad and many others after him have noticed a very different perspective on faith in this literature, in which the usual priority of Israel is not acknowledged. The central figure is an Egyptian power agent and the modes of faith and knowledge are extraordinarily "cool." Indeed, one could imagine that Joseph would have been uncomfortable if he had ever been caught in a conversation behind the wall. Or perhaps that is what the private conversation with the brothers is about (Genesis 45:1–3). Compared with the public function of Joseph, this meeting with the brothers is a hidden, private meeting in which the vulnerability of the man is articulated as it never would be in the public arena. It becomes clear that for Joseph this is a very different conversation, emotionally freighted like the public conversation is not, for it is here that the providential care of YHWH is articulated. Joseph is perhaps a model for keeping two distinct conversations going, which seem not closely related to each other.

2. In the oracles against the nations (Isaiah 13—23; Amos 1—2; Jeremiah 46—51; Ezekiel 25—32), there is a pervasive assumption of YHWH's governance.[29] There are clearly ethical expectations from YHWH that operate at the wall and well outside the wall. YHWH's governance is not coterminous with Israel. As a literary genre, the oracles against the nations make a quite distinct point. In our field of reference, YHWH is at work at the wall, without reference to Israel behind the wall. It is in Amos 2:6–16 that the theology of "YHWH and the nations" functions as a critique of the sectarian tradition. Amos accomplishes this odd turn of the norm by the shrewd move of incorporating Israel among the nations and thereby treating Israel like the other nations, subject to the same expectations. The result is that Israel is judged, not by its covenantal understandings, but as one of the nations without privilege or priority. All the hermeneutical privilege belonging to Israel is nullified by that move. Israel must answer like all the others.

3. In at least two other places, Amos continues this critique. In Amos 3:2, the claim of election is reversed; on this, see Genesis 18:18–19. And in Amos 9:7, the claims of the sectarian narrative are affirmed and made inclusive:

"Are you not like the Ethiopians to me,
    O people of Israel?" says the Lord.
"Did I not bring up Israel from the land of Egypt,
    and the Philistines from Caphtor and the Syrians from Kir?"

The exodus is affirmed. Then it is also affirmed that what seems to be the peculiar property of the community behind the wall is no peculiar property, because YHWH characteristically causes exoduses for many peoples. This is a remarkable intellectual claim, for at the same time the normative claim of the sectarian narrative is affirmed and exploded.[30] It is not argued that the normative claim of the exodus recital is anything but true and normative. It is only asserted that the paradigm of exodus may not be monopolized by Israel for itself. The paradigm may not be kept safely behind the wall.

4. The most remarkable *criticism of a monopolized claim* is found in Isaiah 19:19–25. It is an eschatological vision. But the function of a social vision behind the wall may be twofold. On the face of it, it is a source of hope for a genuinely new thing. But behind that, more subtly, not so obviously but more poignantly, the oracle may be a critique of the hope so fervently held behind the wall. The promise is that the day will come when the theological map of the Near East will look this way:

> In that day Israel will be the third with Egypt and Assyria, a blessing in the midst of the earth, whom the Lord of hosts has blessed, saying, "Blessed be Egypt *my people,* and Assyria *the work of my hands,* and Israel *my heritage.*
> —Isaiah 19:24–25; emphasis added

The ones outside the wall will be reckoned equally along with Israel. The monopoly will be broken. Again, it is worth noting that the new inclusive vision can only be articulated in the language of the sectarian community: *my people/work of my hands/ my heritage.* Even this most inclusive vision in Israel holds to the language and vocabulary of the sect in order to make the point.

5. Finally, *the Isaiah tradition* is notoriously difficult to assess in this as in all matters.[31] The critical problems are acute, because Isaiah 1—39 is so open that it seems to include all sorts of different theological claims.[32] The problems are tradition-critical because it is exceedingly difficult to determine which memories nurture Isaiah, if indeed we could locate the words of that prophet. It seems likely that Isaiah is especially informed by the Zion tradition,[33] perhaps especially those of the enthronement festival (cf. the Psalms) which seem reflected in his call vision. So Isaiah is nurtured in that tendency to assign to the Israelite tradition imperial scope of the most ambitious kind.

But, of course, Isaiah not only *transmits* that uncriticized tradition. He also criticizes it. I will cite only two examples. First, in Isaiah 1:21–26, the whole history of the "protected city" is summarized. It begins in an *initial dream* of justice, righteousness, and faithfulness (v. 21). Then the poem envisions a *dismantling*

(vv. 24–25). And finally the poem promises *renewal* (v. 26). I suppose that the intent of the poem turns on how drastic the second phase is, how deep the judgment cuts. My own evangelical bias is that it cuts very, very deep, but that is a judgment that is not required by the text. Even if not taken with such an accent on discontinuity, what is clear from the entire chapter is that the city behind the wall is not safe and is subject to the rigorous norms of YHWH. Any eighth-century Zionist who imagines this city with a safe-conduct from YHWH has skewed the tradition, as Isaiah understands it.

The other noteworthy text I cite is in 6:9–10, in which it is clear that this people with special access is utterly unresponsive. Anyone who prized the tradition or imagined it gave special insight or sensitivity is uninformed. The judgment leads, in vv. 12–13, to a vision of termination as harsh as the uncreation in Jeremiah 4:23–36. No special privilege.

It can be argued that I have taken the easiest and most obvious examples of how the tradition critiques the tradition. Certainly it is true that the sectarian tradition is not everywhere critiqued. At many points, it is simply trustingly embraced. But the evidence is not only that the sectarian tradition is critiqued. It is critiqued precisely by those who have been, in one way or another, engaged in this other tradition at the wall. In the cases of the YHWHist tradition, Amos and Isaiah, it is the experience at the wall, with the nations, beyond the community, that leads to criticism. Thus the experience behind the wall gives Israel courage on the wall. Conversely, the experience on the wall provides a critique of the community behind the wall which regards itself too exclusively.

V

A series of provisional conclusions may be drawn about this bilingual enterprise before we make some derivative judgments.

1. The heart of the matter is the sectarian narrative. That is not negotiable or in doubt. The primal conversation in the Old Testament is behind the wall, and it is not different in the New Testament. It is a tradition of suspicion against the dominant rationality. It is the witness of the whole tradition, I believe, that

this posture of suspicion is the source of vitality and passion, and I daresay of compassion and humaneness.

2. This sectarian narrative tradition provides the best critical vantage point from which to assess the dominant rationality. This is true not only in the text but as the text has made its way through history. This text stands resiliently in tension with dominant rationality. It is this scandalous text of particularity which has persistently raised questions about the preemptive claims of absolute ideology. It is a topic for another day, but I submit that it is the materiality of this sectarian tradition (mediated by Marx and Freud) that has critiqued every absolutism that is legitimated by ideology, covered over by spiritual mythology and idealism.[34] This critical vantage point for church education is especially important if criticism of ideology is now central to church education rather than construction.

3. But the dominant voice at the wall is not the only one tempted to absolutism. When the conversation behind the wall ignores the other conversation and imagines that it conducts the only conversation, then that conversation behind the wall also becomes ideological and idolatrous. The characteristic way this happens is through an exaggerated attention to "chosenness"; on this, see Matthew 3:7–10.[35]

Then the sectarian tradition needs also to be critiqued. What I have found telling is that the critique is based on two curiously juxtaposed matters. On the one hand, the critique of the sectarian tradition does come from *the awareness of the others* who must be taken seriously on their own terms. But the terms of the critique seem characteristically not to be derived from there. The terms of the critique are found, rather, *within the tradition itself.* Indeed the imperial tradition is no reliable basis for critique, because it is inherently autonomous and is therefore aimed away from YHWH and the accompanying social vision. But apparently the various critiques have had no trouble in using the tradition against the tradition.[36] That is a formal observation about what is done in the text. I submit that this may be substantively important for our common work in church education. What is decisive and definitional in this tradition is its *aniconic* capacity against both conversations, including the one where the tradition itself is the subject under discussion.[37]

4. All of this leads to an unavoidable conclusion, namely, that both conversations are important and good church education must be bilingual. Both must be critiqued on the basis of the claims of the sectarian tradition.

a. It is the liberal temptation, so embarrassed at the sectarian narrative, to believe that the conversation at the wall is the only conversation and that all needs for conversation can be met there. That, of course, is not countenanced by any of the Judean voices in our textual encounter with Assyria. That is, none of those in the story seem like very good liberals. They all know there is another conversation.

b. It is the conservative temptation, so enamored of the sectarian narrative in its uncriticized form, to imagine it is the only conversation and to conclude that anybody who wants conversation at all must join this conversation. I submit that this is the reading made by some Americans from the right of the World Council of Churches, and it seems to be the posture of the Reagan Administration on arms control.

c. The conversation at the wall, conducted according to imperial rationality, is a poor, if not impossible, place in which to do the "night work" of dream and vision, of remembering and hoping, of caring and fearing, of compassion and passion. There the subject is of another kind. It is about companies and quotas of horses and riders (cf. 18:23–24), deadlines and performance. Many burned-out and cynical liberals have succumbed to this conversation as though it were the serious conversation, when, in fact, it cannot by definition be serious about some matters.

d. Conversely, the conversation behind the wall is probably not a suitable or effective place for policy formation. Policy cannot be formed in a vacuum, even though the Reagan Administration carries on this kind of conversation about arms. Policy cannot be formed for great concentrations of power out of a community that only tells stories about its hurts and fears.

e. So our valuing of the sectarian hermeneutic of the Bible seems to me to depend on being clear about the function of this hermeneutic in other conversations. I continue to be fascinated with and convinced by Paul Ricoeur's judgment that change of obedience comes from changed imagination,[38] which characteristically is informed by ambiguity, hurt, and discontinuity. All of that is part of the conversation. Such talk is not irrational, but it is a rationality that grows out of hurt processed, of cries heard, of bread multiplied, of sin forgiven, of the dead raised, and debt canceled and outcasts come home (cf. Luke 4:18–19; 7:22).

It is the intent of this language not only that these folks on the wall will speak and hear and decide differently. It is the hope of this community that the others on the wall who do not speak this language (Hebrew) or share this communal imagination (of the Israelite narrative) will, by this accent used on the wall, be permitted to go back and engage in a conversation behind their wall. There is nothing so impossible on the wall as to have a conversation partner (it matters not from which side) who has no conversation going on elsewhere which processes the sordid and surging realities of humanness. If the conversation at the wall is the only conversation in which one participates, that conversation becomes too serious, one-dimensional,[39] with too much at stake and nothing left for negotiation, maneuverability, or disclosure. If one is not involved in a conversation of criticism and freedom, then the public discussion must inevitably be marked by an absence of self-criticism, freedom, and a sense of humor. Very quickly everything becomes necessary.

VI

It remains now to relate this to the terms of our more general discussion. Our topic remains "the legitimacy of a sectarian hermeneutic."

1. It is clear that a hermeneutic is not only necessary but inevitable. There are no raw events.[40] There are only events shaped and discerned through a community of perception. It is not excessively reductionist to say, in this context, that the options available are limited to a perception from those on the wall which absolutizes the dominant rationality, or an interpretation from behind the wall which is porous and contains the capacity for self-criticism. A hermeneutic there must be; and without the intentionality of the sectarian community, the dominant rationality will claim the field at high costs to our humanness.

2. We ask if the conversation behind the wall is legitimate. The criterion we have set is this: Does it hold together the reality of *experience*, the necessary functions of *administration*, and the expressive *symbols* which claim, assert, and guarantee energy? The answer in the text itself is "yes." We do not presume to go behind the text to "what happened." What the text presents as having happened is that the conversation behind the wall (consisting in penance, prayer, and oracle) completely changed the conversation on the wall. That conversation behind the wall did touch real public experience, did cope with administrative crisis, and did generate newness. We can agree that this is a very "odd" text,[41] and this is surely no way to conduct foreign policy. Indeed we might say it was a "miracle," and one cannot build policy on miracles.

To this I make these responses:

- We are trying to study a text and not an event behind the text. If we take the text as text, it carves out for us a moment to "reread" reality differently.
- I suppose it is always a "miracle" when the conversation behind the wall decisively impinges on the conversation at the wall. Or, said another way, it is a miracle when the imagination of the community can break the dominant rationality. I daresay that miraculous turns are in fact what church education is about.
- I intend, in terms of legitimacy, that this conversation behind the wall be judged not by its power to form policy but by its capacity to transform imagination, which makes a differently textured policy possible. Our scientific, objective, historical-critical ways have a difficulty in letting the text do its proper work, without a demand that it do some other work, perhaps more palatable to our rationality.[42]
- The text is an oddity. Indeed it is such an oddity that the tradition of Israel included it twice. So I do not suggest that its impingement on imagination should be treated as routine, normal, or capable of replication. It does seem, however, that the notion of an "oddity" is of the crucial substance for our faith community and its educational processes.

On all these counts, I regard the conversation behind the wall as legitimate, as having decisively changed the other conversation which appears to the world to be the decisive one.

3. The sectarian character of this story is evident. It belongs to

this language group with this memory. Two dimensions are important. First, that it belongs to this minority community is definitional. It cannot be any other way. Imperial regimes do not tell tales of slave escapes. So unless we are to abandon the substance, we must accept the fact of sectarianism. Roman governors do not jest at resurrections (cf. Matthew 28:14), Jerusalem kings do not bow down at mangers (cf. Matthew 2:13). It belongs to the genre and subject matter to be sectarian. But second, the nerve of this tradition behind the wall is to insist that this tale is "porous" enough that it will touch the experience of others if they will climb down off the wall to tell stories in their community of hurt and passion. That is, the governing miracles are common to all human persons in all human communities, even though some have long ago opted for imperial ideology.

So, I conclude that the sectarian interpretation is legitimate, because (a) it offers a reading of reality which claims assent and (b) it provides an alternative to an imperial rationality that nullifies the very subject matter of this interpretation.

Finally, some comments about the practice of interpretation. As I said earlier, programmatically and theoretically, church education should aim at both tasks, *the language of policy formation and the language of transformative imagination*. There is merit in seeing these as distinct tasks but dependent upon each other. (Thus, I regard the *Christian Education: Shared Approaches* curriculum[43] arrangement of choosing between these language systems as pernicious.)

But when I consider our particular *social situation* and the *church constituency* we reach, I conclude that the conversation behind the wall with its capacity for self-criticism needs particular attention:

- Concerning church constituency in broad sweep, it is the church constituency of middle America that most vigorously supports the inhuman policies of our government. Our educational access is not to government leaders who form policy but to the public which permits, authorizes, and embraces policy. Education for such a constituency needs to be not so much the technicalities of policy questions (i.e., what should be said at the wall) as a transformed imagination, informed by hurt, ambiguity, and discontinuity.

- The self-critical capacity of that tradition is urgent when a goodly portion of church constituency on the right handles the sectarian interpretation of tradition without a shred of suspicion. I do not believe that education in conversation at the wall is what is needed, but address to the frightened assembly that holds these close narratives one-dimensionally.
- There is a confusion and collapse of the two stories now sadly evident in Robert Schuller and in civil religion generally. Neither story has an integrity, but the reasons of state are all intertwined with affairs of the heart, and neither can be critiqued or discerned clearly.
- In the liberal church, so captured by laudable goals and imperial methods, the story that has lost power is the one behind the walls. And so, we end up with more knowledge about what to do, but without the will, courage, energy, or self-knowledge to act. What is required, then, is a sectarian tale that gives us freedom against our perceived vested interest.

This is not a plea for withdrawal or obscurantism, or a disregard of conversation at the wall where policy must be formed in the presence of the wielders of power. But it grows out of my sense of the real crisis among us. It is a crisis of legitimacy. At the moment, my sense is that we have forgotten our primal language. Other languages are pressed in their place. Aramaic sounds a lot like Hebrew, but only the Assyrian ambassador thought it was equivalent. The folks who knew both languages could identify the foreign accent and could identify the difference.

NOTES

1. Brevard S. Childs, *Isaiah and the Assyrian Crisis*, Studies in Biblical Theology, Second Series, no. 3 (Naperville, Ill.: Alec R. Allenson, 1967). See Childs's later summary of the general issues in his *Introduction to the Old Testament as Scripture* (Philadelphia: Fortress Press, 1979), pp. 318–25. See also the important work of Ronald E. Clements, *Isaiah and the Deliverance of Jerusalem*, Journal for the Study of the Old Testament—Supplement Series, no. 13 (Sheffield, Eng.: JSOT Press, 1980).
2. One of the freedoms exercised at the wall by those who have another conversation elsewhere is the freedom not to answer and so not

30 WALTER BRUEGGEMANN

to enlist in the dominant rationality. See Daniel 3:16–18; John 18:8–11. On the latter, see Paul L. Lehmann, *The Transfiguration of Politics* (New York: Harper & Row, 1975), pp. 48–78. Note esp. p. 68.

3. See the most helpful summary by Anthony C. Thiselton, *The Two Horizons* (Grand Rapids, Mich.: Wm. B. Eerdmans Publishing Co., 1980). In what follows, it will be evident that I am influenced particularly by Paul Ricoeur.

4. Ernst Troeltsch, *The Social Teaching of the Christian Churches*, 2 vols. (New York: Macmillan Co., 1931). Troeltsch's summary statement is: "The sect is a voluntary society, composed of strict and definite Christian believers bound to each other by the fact that all have experienced 'the new birth.' These 'believers' live apart from the world, are limited to small groups, emphasize the law instead of grace, and in varying degrees within their own circle set up the Christian order, based on love; all this is done in preparation for and expectation of the coming kingdom of God" (II: 993). In what follows, it will be clear that I have taken important liberties with this characterization. It remains to be seen whether my improvisations completely distort the question under discussion.

5. H. Richard Niebuhr, *The Social Sources of Denominationalism* (New York: Henry Holt & Co., 1929), esp. pp. 17–21.

6. The language, of course, is derived from Peter L. Berger and Thomas Luckmann, *The Social Construction of Reality: A Treatise in the Sociology of Knowledge* (Garden City, N.Y.: Doubleday & Co., 1966). But see especially Berger's earlier book, *The Precarious Vision* (Garden City, N.Y.: Doubleday & Co., 1961). Berger's analysis there is about a protected construction of reality jeopardized by more expansive experience. The theme is not unrelated to sectarianism.

7. See Elisabeth Schüssler Fiorenza, *In Memory of Her: A Feminist Theological Reconstruction of Christian Origins* (New York: Crossroad, 1983), for a history of pain which has almost been completely lost to us because of a censored reading of the text.

8. Eric W. Gritsch and Robert W. Jenson, *Lutheranism: The Theological Movement and Its Confessional Writings* (Philadelphia: Fortress Press, 1976), chap. 1, have suggested, for example, that the Lutheran Confessions are an offer made by the Lutheran community to the whole church. When it is no longer a proposal but an ultimatum (which, of course, Jenson does not intend), then it becomes a destructive monopoly.

9. On "the living God," see Siegfried Kreuzer, *Der lebendige Gott*, Beiträge zur Wissenschaft vom Alten und Neuen Testament, no. 116 (Stuttgart: W. Kohlhammer, 1983); and Hans-Joachim Kraus, "The Living God: A Chapter of Biblical Theology," in *Theology of the Liberating Word*, ed. Frederick Herzog (New York: Abingdon Press, 1971), pp. 76–107.

10. The original sociological work on this subject is that of Max Weber. But Jürgen Habermas has considerably advanced the discussion. See Jürgen Habermas, *Legitimation Crisis* (Boston: Beacon Press, 1975), esp. pt. II, chap. 6. See also Peter Berger, *The Sacred Canopy: Elements of a Sociological Theory of Religion* (Garden City, N.Y.: Doubleday & Co., 1967), esp. pp. 32–39.

11. Habermas, *Legitimation Crisis*, p. 70.

12. On false symbols as ways of social control, see Jacques Ellul, *Propaganda: The Formation of Men's Attitudes* (New York: Alfred A. Knopf, 1965). On the failure of symbols, see Robert J. Lifton in his various analyses of the "symbol gap."

13. See Alvin W. Gouldner, *The Coming Crisis of Western Sociology* (New York: Basic Books, 1970), which concerns failed objectivity in the social sciences as an illegitimate enterprise. See also Berger, *The Sacred Canopy*, pp. 90–92; and Habermas, *Legitimation Crisis*, pp. 73, 93. Gary A. Herion, "The Social Organization of Tradition in Monarchic Judah" (Ph.D. diss., University of Michigan, 1982), p. 59 and passim, has shown that only conformity is required, not assent, by the administrators of the dominant rationality.

14. On bureaucratic use of an expressive symbol, see Walter Brueggemann, " 'Vine and Fig Tree': A Case Study in Imagination and Criticism," *Catholic Biblical Quarterly* 43 (1981): 188–204.

15. On the power of such primal speech to change worlds, see Peter L. Berger, *A Rumor of Angels* (Garden City, N.Y.: Doubleday & Co., 1970), pp. 54–56.

16. Wayne A. Meeks, *The First Urban Christians: The Social World of the Apostle Paul* (New Haven: Yale University Press, 1983), has shown how the Pauline corpus in the New Testament is almost completely concerned with the internal ordering and symbolization of the community or, in our terms, with the conversation behind the wall.

17. See the very shrewd discernment of this factor by Herbert N. Schneidau, *Sacred Discontent: The Bible and Western Tradition* (Baton Rouge: Louisiana State University Press, 1976), and the ongoing sociocultural function of that critical dimension.

18. Norman K. Gottwald, *The Tribes of Yahweh: A Sociology of the Religion of Liberated Israel 1250–1050 B.C.E.* (Maryknoll, N.Y.: Orbis Books, 1979).

19. See Johannes Pedersen, *Israel: Its Life and Culture*, vols. 3–4 (London: Oxford University Press, 1940), pp. 728–37.

20. Michael Fishbane, *Text and Texture: Close Readings of Selected Biblical Texts* (New York: Schocken Books, 1979), pp. 79–83, has observed the problematic dimension of this transmission from generation to generation.

21. See Walter Harrelson, "Life, Faith and the Emergence of Tradi-

tion," in *Tradition and Theology in the Old Testament*, ed. Douglas A. Knight (Philadelphia: Fortress Press, 1977), pp. 11–30.

22. For a remarkable analysis of the pathology of totalitarian voices and the way of recovering healthy speech, see Eugen Rosenstock-Huessy, *The Origin of Speech* (Norwich, Vt.: Argo Books, 1981).

23. The seminal study of Martin Buber, *Kingship of God* (New York: Harper & Row, 1967), anticipated much of what has come later with regard to the political power of this metaphor. In some ways, Buber has anticipated the entire development of Mendenhall and Gottwald, though not, of course, expressed in those terms.

24. See Mendenhall's summary of his analysis in "The Conflict Between Value Systems and Social Control," in *Unity and Diversity: Essays in the History, Literature, and Religion of the Ancient Near East*, ed. Hans Goedicke and J.J.M. Roberts (Baltimore: Johns Hopkins University Press, 1975), pp. 169–80.

25. Paul D. Hanson, "The Theological Significance of Contradiction Within the Book of the Covenant," *Canon and Authority: Essays in Old Testament Religion and Theology*, ed. George W. Coats and Burke O. Long (Philadelphia: Fortress Press, 1977), pp. 110–31.

26. One can argue that as the early period tended to be capable of such an intentional social organization which may be regarded as sectarian, so in the later postexilic period the same possibility emerged. Thus the social reform of Nehemiah in Nehemiah 5 bears many of the same marks as the initial intentionality of Moses.

27. Norbert Lohfink, *Great Themes from the Old Testament* (Edinburgh: T. & T. Clark, 1982), pp. 55–75, has indicated that the legal materials of Deuteronomy are in fact intentional about administrative reality and finds traces of a "constitution" for a social organization.

28. Hans Walter Wolff, "The Kerygma of the Yahwist," in *The Vitality of Old Testament Traditions*, ed. Walter Brueggemann and Hans Walter Wolff (Atlanta: John Knox Press, 1975), pp. 41–66.

29. The best critical study of these texts is that of Norman K. Gottwald, *All the Kingdoms of the Earth: Israelite Prophecy and Industrial Relations in the Ancient Near East* (New York: Harper & Row, 1964).

30. Walther Zimmerli, *I Am Yahweh* (Atlanta: John Knox Press, 1982), has shown in a series of articles that the authoritative base for YHWHism is found in the self-disclosure of YHWH in a formula that belongs in the sectarian community. The intent of YHWH's actions is that "the nations may know." But the formulae that comment on the acts are formulae that have their setting and sense in the closer community.

31. Herion, "Social Organization," pp. 312–21, has shown how the tradition of Isaiah is a remarkable "blending" of the voices we are seeking to identify.

32. On the complexity of the Isaiah tradition as it came to contain

many voices, see Ronald E. Clements, *Isaiah 1—39,* New Century Bible Commentary (Grand Rapids, Mich.: Wm. B. Eerdmans Publishing Co., 1980), who is especially influenced by the hypotheses of Hermann Barth, *Die Jesaja-Worte in der Jusiazeit* (Neukirchen-Vluyn: Neukircherner Verlag, 1977).

33. See Gerhard von Rad, *Old Testament Theology,* vol. 2 (London: Oliver & Boyd, 1965), pp. 147–75.

34. This is why Gottwald's proposal is so important. See Gottwald, *The Tribes of Yahweh,* pp. 592–607, on the problematic of an idealist reading. More positively on a materialist reading, see Kuno Fussel, "The Materialist Reading of the Bible," in *The Bible and Liberation: Politics and Social Hermeneutics,* ed. Norman K. Gottwald (Maryknoll, N.Y.: Orbis Books, 1983), pp. 134–64; Fernando Belo, *A Materialist Reading of the Gospel of Mark* (Maryknoll, N.Y.: Orbis Books, 1981), especially the introductory materials; and Walter J. Hollenweger, "The Other Exegesis," *Horizons in Biblical Theology* 3 (1981): 155–79.

35. It is a pervasive judgment that in recent Old Testament theology, too much attention has been paid to the more sectarian traditions to the neglect of more comprehensive claims. A number of scholars have made proposals to redress that one-sided approach, including Paul Hanson, Samuel Terrien, and Claus Westermann. See my article "A Convergence in Recent Old Testament Theologies," *Journal for the Study of the Old Testament* 18 (1980): 2–18.

36. See Walter Zimmerli, "Prophetic Proclamation and Reinterpretation," in Knight, *Tradition and Theology in the Old Testament,* pp. 69–100, and more programmatically Schneidau, *Sacred Discontent.*

37. On the *aniconic* character of the tradition, see John Dominic Crossan, *Finding Is the First Act* (Philadelphia: Fortress Press, 1979), pp. 93–122.

38. Paul Ricoeur, "Toward a Hermeneutic of the Idea of Revelation," in *Essays on Biblical Interpretation,* ed. Lewis S. Mudge (Philadelphia: Fortress Press, 1980). That judgment has been worked out in some detail as concerns education by Craig Dykstra, *Vision and Character: A Christian Educator's Alternative to Kohlberg* (New York: Paulist Press, 1981).

39. See Herbert Marcuse, *One Dimensional Man: Studies in the Ideology of Advanced Industrial Society* (Boston: Beacon Press, 1966), esp. chap. 4, where he describes the dominant language as becoming so narrow and coercive that it no longer permits serious communication.

40. See the judicious way in which Amos N. Wilder, "Story and Story-World," *Interpretation* 37 (1983): 353–64, has sorted out this matter. He places major stress on the creative power of narrative construction, but in a way that is not subjectivist.

41. On the "oddity" of the text as a way of revelation, see Paul Ricoeur, "Biblical Hermeneutics," *Semeia* 4 (1975): 122–29. Such "oddity"

belongs to its revelatory power.

42. See my brief consideration of this problem in "The Text Makes Sense," *The Christian Ministry* 14 (November 1983): 7–10.

43. *Christian Education: Shared Approaches*, produced during 1978–88, was a project of Joint Educational Development, a consortium of Protestant demoninations.

2

The Two Pedagogies: Discipleship and Citizenship

John A. Coleman

My focus in this essay is on the role of the church in educating for discipleship and citizenship. Both of these main topics are too large, complex, and multifaceted to be encompassed in one mere essay. Thus, of necessity, what follows will contain abbreviated formulae, truncated arguments and theses, some of them quite controversial. The essay contains eight subtopics:

1. Citizenship and Discipleship
2. The Meaning of Discipleship
3. The Meaning of Citizenship
4. Neighbor and Social Companion: Citizenship and Discipleship as Two Semiautonomous but Interrelated Zones
5. What Citizenship Adds to Discipleship: A Wider Solidarity, a Humbler Service, a New Reality Test for Responsibility
6. What Discipleship Adds to Citizenship: Utopia, Counterculture, Vocation
7. Some Central New Testament Texts on Citizenship and Ethics: Mark 12:13–17; Romans 13:1–7

8. Educating for Citizenship-Discipleship: *Vamos Caminando: A Peruvian Catechism*[1]

Introduction: Three Theses

I propose three major theses concerning discipleship and citizenship. First, each concept points to semiautonomous yet interrelated zones of life. It should come as no surprise that, from both sides, there exists an irreducible tension between the moral practices and demands of citizenship and discipleship.

In sections 1, 2, and 3 of this essay on the *aporiae* (i.e., the perpetually unresolvable tensions or problematics) of citizenship and discipleship, I will explore some of these tensions, suggest the meanings of the two terms, and give some reasons why the two zones are both semiautonomous (neither reducible to nor subordinated to the other) yet interrelated. In a summary way I will be attempting to state the correlation between what Paul Ricoeur has called the two pedagogies: the pedagogy of power and the pedagogy of nonviolent discipleship.[2] Behind this notion of the two pedagogies lies the classical ethical dialectic postulated by Max Weber, who spoke of a tension between an ethics of responsibility (for political life) and the ethics of absolute ends typified by the Sermon on the Mount.

Second, my thesis is that the church that educates for discipleship must also concern itself with education for citizenship. As I see it, worldly address and social-political responsibility are constitutive demands of church membership. In section 4, by focusing on the three notions of ecclesial utopia, evangelical counterculture, and constructive vocation, I will be defending my third thesis, succinctly worded by D.W.Brogan in his book of essays, *Citizenship Today:* "A Christian citizen has more duties than and different from those that the state defines and demands."[3]

Sections 5 and 6 assume a genuine dialectic between discipleship and citizenship. In section 7, I signal several sets of central New Testament texts concerning citizenship: Romans 13:1–7 (which needs *always* to be juxtaposed with Revelation 13), Mark 12:13–17 on tax tribute to Caesar, and Pauline texts on New Testament ethics. In this section I will maintain that Romans 13:1–7, read in its full context, confirms Brogan's thesis that

Christian citizens have more duties than the state defines. They must exercise their citizenship precisely as discipleship, "in the Lord," thus transforming the meaning of citizenship. I will also maintain that Christian ethics always presupposes, as the ground material on which it works toward transformation, an already given cultural ethic. In modern society this is the ethics of citizenship.

Finally, in section 8, I will look very briefly at one relatively successful attempt to relate the concepts of citizenship-discipleship in church education: *Vamos Caminando: A Peruvian Catechism*, compiled by the pastoral team of Bambamarca, a city in the northern Andes of Peru.

I am more than aware that in a society as religiously pluralistic as the United States, my way of construing the relationship between discipleship and citizenship will not mirror other Christian choices. I opt for an account that combines, in some tension, H. Richard Niebuhr's Christ against culture and Christ transforming culture models, mirroring the New Testament tension between Paul and the Johannine Revelation.[4] I have not tried to speak of a unitary Judeo-Christian view for several reasons. Discipleship is not a general Jewish ethical concept. Although Christians feel bound to the Hebrew scriptures as constitutive of their self-understanding, many from the Jewish community resent the term a Judeo-Christian ethic as patronizing or a species of Christian imperialism.

As these remarks make clear, the moral concept of citizenship in a religiously pluralistic world will have to be based on a wider notion than discipleship—probably, at root, on a nontheological understanding of the rights and duties of membership in the commonwealth or the tradition of civic republican virtue. As Robin Lovin has sanely remarked, "Theological affirmations make poor premises for public moral arguments because they are held by a limited group of the faithful."[5] I agree fully with Robert Bellah and his associates in their *Habits of the Heart* that a renewal of both discipleship and the more secular notion of republican virtue in the classic concept of republican citizenship would be necessary for any vital public philosophy in America today, although I do not give the two notions the equal weight they give them.[6]

1. Citizenship and Discipleship

In his book *The Machiavellian Moment* (1975), J.G. Pocock comments that the saints almost always wear their mantle of citizenship lightly. No earthly home mirrors the New Jerusalem. Michael Walzer catches this tension between saints and citizens when he claims for citizenship, almost in relief, that "the standards are not all that high; we are required to be brethren and citizens, not saints and heroes."[7] Even more strongly, from the perspective of the Christian moral ideal of discipleship, the alternative morality of citizenship often contains serious temptations. Hence my initial thesis: there is an irreducible tension between citizenship and discipleship.

To begin with, every politics, undeniably, includes a potentially demonic charismatic ingredient. Hitler and Stalin were not pure aberrations, mere sports in history. As Plato argues in his *Gorgias*, power and sophistry, tyranny and flattery, might and untruth usually march hand in hand. Moreover, at crucial points, effective political power needs mastery over secrecy and control over the techniques that shape consensus and public opinion. Effective state action for the common good demands a certain centralization and concentration of power to ensure decisiveness and direction. Concentrated power, however, inevitably resists the needed participatory access that controls, monitors, and checks abuses of power, so that power can be used to further the common good rather than particular interest. If ever Christian disciples reconcile themselves to citizenship, *in an actually functioning state*, it could only be with some critical and serious reserve.

Like God, politics can be, at times, powerful, creative, willfully decisive, character-shaping, nation-forming, an active agent in history. It determines collective destinies, teleologies, and purposes. Emile Durkheim may have been incorrect in, seemingly, equating God and society, but his insight concerning the godlike control over citizens' lives by society captures a decisive reality—and perennial temptation—of the polis. As the French political philosopher Bertrand de Jouvenel remarks in his classic, *On Power*, power obeys the law of the Minotaur.[8] Ever expansive, indeed sometimes devouring, power seeks, like a god, to become all-powerful. For the Christian, every politics courts idolatry, the displacement of the sovereign God by a sovereign collective societal purpose (a "general will" which, heretofore at least, has almost always been exercised, disproportionately, by a particular elite group within the commonwealth). A maxim suspicious of the political but appropriate to discipleship thus runs, following Lord Acton: Power corrupts and absolute power corrupts absolutely.

The inescapable political temptation toward narrow patriotism or uncritical nationalism stands in stark contradiction to universalism—a God who sits in judgment over *all* nations, including our own. For Christians, by definition, no nation can function as their only home and matrix of culture.

Paul Ricoeur has decisively caught the primary tension between citizenship and discipleship in several of his essays on political ethics, especially in his extraordinarily evocative essay "The Paradox of Power."[9] Ricoeur notes that state political power, in its actual constitution and exercise, almost always took its origin out of violence (war, revolution). Moreover, state political power includes a paradoxical mixture of violence and rationality in its ongoing operation and enjoys a monopoly control over violence so as to sanction the legitimacy of its political decisions. It stands ever poised to resort to violence, if need be, through army or police force, judges, law courts, and prison guards.

As Ricoeur sees it, the paradox of political power, rooted in and relying on violence, has been that it nevertheless represents an instrument of genuine historical rationality and justice. Yet, as Ricoeur notes, the element of rationality in power remains partly extrinsic. As he sees it, power, strangely, knows no history. The crude mechanism of tyranny is as likely to appear in the twentieth century—often more brutally because of advances in technical rationality—as in the first or the sixteenth.[10] Equally paradoxical, membership in a nation-state or a people is necessary for the development of culture, a sense of self and collective purpose. If deprived permanently of political membership and access to power, one is deprived as well of any deep sense of oneself, of a decent self-regard. This has prompted a number of twentieth-century politicians and writers to reverse the famous

Acton maxim to read: Power corrupts, but the lack of power corrupts absolutely.

In the modern state, the decisive central governing organs exercise commanding control to shape, limit, and, in boundary situations, totally control information, the media, ideology, and the worldview of its citizens. This seems, whatever the important differences in degree, as true of the administered state in democratic regimes as in authoritarian societies. This has led many thoughtful Christian observers to fear the loss, corruption, leveling, or co-optation of the distinctively Christian moral voice of discipleship. They fear its total incorporation into the ongoing cultural project of citizenship. Hence, the frequent cries of a cultural captivity of the churches, a watering down of the heady Christian wine.

These authors, such as Stanley Hauerwas and Richard John Neuhaus, are concerned about a blurring of the distinctive face of discipleship by too close amalgamation of discipleship to citizenship. They endorse a version of Dietrich Bonhoeffer's notion of the necessity of a "secret discipline" of discipleship, that is, a discipline that is not publicly, societally controlled, although—it should be noted—in another sense this discipline is public. This secret discipline, the pedagogy of discipleship, takes shape in specifically ecclesial prayer, community, moral discernment and discourse, action, and service and worship. Without such internal church discipline as a counterpedagogy to the societal project the danger remains acute that the church's voice will be neither distinctive nor, in any specific sense, Christian. It will, instead, be a mere echo of the culturally prevalent voice.[11]

Finally, a substantive vision of human life and society subsists in the notion of discipleship. Christians see themselves, however fallibly, following, indeed rendering present in history, the dictates of God's purposes for creation. In some sense, however nuanced and attenuated, they imagine themselves as partaking in "the will of God." Christians assume that discipleship includes a substantive—not merely procedural—view of the social good (embracing, e.g., peace based on justice; the rights of the poor; a specific sense of freedom which is not license; the image of God's covenant justice which vindicates the most marginal).

They propose a determined anthropology of the human being as God's image. In this vision, social goods have a substantive and determinate content related to the biblical utopian concept of the realm of God. Disciples are neither agnostics nor "repressively tolerant" of every competing definition of the social good or the *humanum*. Even granted a certain humility among some Christians concerning the extent to which they have any detailed knowledge of the social good, in general complete agnosticism in these matters would be totally foreign to the Christian tradition.

Notoriously, democracies are agnostic. Democratic citizenship, it is usually argued, must be blind to all substantive arguments concerning social goods. Fair procedure, equal access, societal peace and consensus, the art of the possible take precedence over substantive visions. As Michael Walzer puts it, "The state does not nourish souls." He hastens to add, "Nor does it kill them."[12] It is an axiom of modern democratic government that governments cannot adjudicate between truth claims, whether religious or secular. In Elizabeth I's fine phrase, "The government may not build windows into men's [or women's] souls." This decisive division between the moral ideals of citizenship and discipleship entails a permanent distinction between any community of disciples and a genuinely political and democratic commonwealth of citizens.

On the other hand, history attests to the dangers and societal destructiveness of Catholic authoritarian state rule in the name of divine sanction or a Calvinist rule of the saints. The Inquisition, Calvin's Geneva, Puritan New England, and Cromwell's England rightly lack effective contemporary champions. We have learned, at great cost, to decide, against Cromwell, that divine grace carries no specific political weight. Again, Walzer states the point succinctly:

> Democracy is a way of allocating power and legitimating its use. . . . Every extrinsic reason is ruled out. What counts is argument among the citizens. Democracy puts a premium on speech, persuasion, rhetorical skill. Ideally, the citizen who makes the most persuasive argument—that is, the argument that actually persuades the largest number of citizens—get his [or her] way. . . . It is not only the inclusiveness, however, that makes for democratic

government. Equally important is what we might call the rule of reasons. Citizens come into the forum with nothing but their arguments. All non-political goods have to be deposited outside: weapons and wallets, titles and degrees.[13]

And, I would add, "creeds or ethics of discipleship." As Walzer trenchantly notes, "If enough people are committed to the rule of the saints, then the saints should have no difficulty winning elections."[14] The game of citizenship constrains the saints' language system. *Whatever their background revelational foundation, disciples can make their case as citizens only in a discourse of secular warrant and public reason.* Clearly a realm of pluralistic "values," life aims, and discourse is but a pale shadow of the reign of God. For this reason, as Walter Brueggemann argues in his essay in this volume, disciples need to be bilingual to translate their appropriate language into the categories of citizenship.

Christian theorists of discipleship have complained, then, of the leveling character of this ideal of citizenship, its introduction of a relative notion of morality or truth into the common life (perhaps, even, its claim to permit, for the sake of common life or peaceful consensus, behavior that the disciple judges repugnant and seriously sinful). The rules of the game of citizenship substitute an arena of *opinion* for an arena of substantive truth. Some disciples see and decry this citizen arena as a purely "naked public square."[15]

Theorists of citizenship, for their part, have not lacked legitimate complaints about the deleterious intrusion of the ideal of discipleship into the commonwealth of citizens. The brutal and passionate wars of religion spawned the Enlightenment ideals of secular reason and religious tolerance. Even today, Northern Ireland, India, and Iran can serve as case examples of the violence and dangers of sectarian religious politics.

The litany of complaints against the intrusion of discipleship into citizenship reaches back to Roman times. A typical rebuke—voiced strongly by Rousseau—is that the Christian ideal of a universal solidarity undercuts urgent commitment to *this* particular nationally defined sovereignty and general will. Alexis de Tocqueville captures Rousseau's complaint in these comments:

Christianity and consequently its morality went beyond all political power and nationalities. Its grand achievement is to have formed a human community beyond national societies. The duties of men among themselves as well as their capacity as citizens, the duties of citizens to their fatherland, in brief, the public virtues, seem to me to have been inadequately defined and considerably neglected within the moral system of Christianity.

To his administrative assistant, Arthur de Gobineau, Tocqueville remarked, "Because the French clergy emphasizes only private morality, the nation at large has not been taught the duties of citizenship."[16]

It seems to me that Tocqueville is right; it is undeniable that Christianity lacks a coherent, fully developed, Christian theory of citizenship, a specifically Christian sense of any sacredness or vocational meaning of membership in a particular nation with its own national character type and historic goals and challenges.

Other complaints by citizens to the disciples, besides this Tocquevillean rebuke of privatization—as if personal honesty, truth telling, promise keeping, or sexual integrity exhaust or even adequately express a truly *public* morality—have noted the otherworldliness of the Christian ideal, its lack of seriousness about the historically contingent. For their part, the Marxists have documented the ideological misuses of religion to compensate the suffering of the poor or to legitimate the wealth of the dominant. A final rebuke notes the way Romans 13:1–7 has, generally, been interpreted to legitimate a mere dutiful citizenship, a Lutheran two-kingdom passive obedience rather than that more active, critical engagement of citizen-politicians espoused eloquently by Michael Walzer. As Walzer contends, "The citizen/voter is crucial to the survival of democratic politics; but the citizen/politician is crucial to its liveliness and integrity."[17]

Power is ambiguous. It remains an inscrutable reality and, inexorably, a force both for rationality, equality, and personal empowerment or enhancement and, as well, for violence, manipulation, and domination. Generally, Christian theorists of discipleship either avoid the issue of power, lament it, and point exclusively to its dangers or restrict themselves to a pedagogy of nonviolence not fully coherent with the political, the realm of power and possibility within constrained contingency. Like the theology of citizenship, a developed theology of power is conspicuously lacking in the libraries or minds of most disciples. This lack led Max Weber to postulate a stark—almost unbridgeable—division between an ethics of discipleship and an ethics of power, between disciples and citizens.

Paul Ricoeur, who exhibits much sympathy for Weber's dilemma, states again the core of this *aporia* between citizenship and discipleship.

> It is not responsible (and is even impossible) to deduce a politics from a theology. This is so because every political involvement grows out of a truly secular set of information, a situational arena which proffers a limited field of possible actions and available means, and a more or less risk-taking option, a gamble, among these possibilities.[18]

Politics remains more art than science, an art, moreover, exercised in a world not yet redeemed and transformed by grace in that paradoxical arena which mingles coercive dominance and violence with rationality and justice. The disciple neither knows better than the unbeliever nor necessarily loves more that truly political common good which might be genuinely possible.

From the Christian vantage point, both a theology of citizenship (as membership in a limited, historically contingent nation-state community) and a theology of power remain as glaring lacunae for any project of correlation between discipleship and citizenship. Both the nature of power (as a paradoxical mixture of violence and rational justice) and the nature of the political (as shaped by a conjuncture of intractable forces, movements, boundaries, and limited, even at times determinate, possibilities) suggest that no simple formula in either praxis or theory will ever truly remove the *aporia* tension between citizenship and discipleship. Perhaps—just perhaps—as Max Weber once hinted in his classic essay on politics as a vocation, there may be moments when the tension between an ethics of discipleship and an ethics of responsible citizenship yields to a creative historical fusion. Between those moments, however, we do well to define our terms and map the two as decidedly separate terrains and life games.

2. The Meaning of Discipleship

Christian discipleship takes on a narrative form. One models the Christian life on (1) the decisive dispositions of Jesus (e.g., surrender to God, gratitude, readiness for service and self-sacrificing love, a preferential option for the poor); (2) crucial paradigmatic actions in Jesus' life (the cross, foot washing, prayer, outreach to those excluded from the community, healing, forgiveness, love of enemies, consistent nonviolence); and (3) a utopian teaching related to the realm of God (e.g., the Sermon on the Mount) caught in parables, narratives, and teaching sayings. Discipleship involves a *paideia* pedagogy of assimilation to the pattern of the nonviolent life and spirit of the teacher who serves as model.

In no way, however, does discipleship entail a mere mechanical imitation of the historical Jesus. Discipleship implies a metanormative ethic. That is, an ethics of discipleship attempts to differentiate norm from context and to apply, in a completely new context, the normative paradigms or models of a life rather than specific culturally bound norms or mores. Discipleship is primarily a "way" and a praxis, rooted in a determined past historical life, to be sure, but meant to transform present lives and structures.

Christianity conceives of itself as a praxis, that is, "The Way." The praxis of following Jesus must mediate between the past historical life of the person, Jesus, as contained, in some sense, in the Gospel narratives, on the one hand, and, on the other, present discernment of analogical parallels to the model of Jesus' (historically and contextually limited) unrepeatable life. As Jon Sobrino has noted, for the Christian imagination, the Christ of faith continues to act in history. "To say that Christ ceases to unleash a Christian reality and a Christian history is formally to deny that he is a Christ."[19] The Christian expects the decisively new in history. Moreover, the pedagogy of discipleship is also

future-oriented. "Christological reflection must be oriented toward the future of God and [God's] kingdom."[20]

The narrative structures concerning the life and teaching of
Jesus keep an ethics of discipleship from remaining a merely
empty cipher capable of taking on any possible content. The
narrative and teaching highlight and prompt toward certain
directions, dispositions, and actions and interdict others. Discipleship today means "discerning the signs of the times," that is,
reading in present events significant analogues for which the
character, life, and teachings of Jesus serve as model, as well as
the future directionality of discipleship where the reign of God
stands as paradigm for *every* human community (not only the
church). Thus, discipleship cannot be legitimately reduced to a
fundamentalist, slavish imitation of the historically situated
Jesus. An effective pedagogy of discipleship thus roots itself in
ethical model-thinking, alert to the historical-contextual specificity of Jesus' time, culture, and society as well as to our own. An
ethics of discipleship presupposes the well-known tensive sense
of eschatology-messianism (the famous "already and not-yet"
arrival of the reign of God). The not-yet character of this es-
chatology creates dissatisfaction with a secure repose in any
ethics of the presently politically possible, of mere compromise,
consensus. Inescapably, an ethics of discipleship contains
idealistic, utopian elements which no actual church community,
let alone political society, can enact.

An ethics of discipleship involves, then, a *paideia* pedagogy of
assimilation and reappropriation—not mere reproduction—of
Jesus' human dispositions, actions, character, and way. Jesus'
way involves a generous covenant response to God's love and
will. As Jon Sobrino persuasively contends, this father of Jesus is
not an abstract, horizon concept but precisely the God of the
idealized kingdom covenant in Jewish messianic and apocalyp-
tic thought.[21] In Jesus' life, that kingdom and covenant enter
history as humanly realized. Jürgen Moltmann notes that for the
Christian the kingdom of God is rendered present in history
precisely by the praxis of the followers of Jesus.[22] "The Way"
involves putting into practice the ideals of that kingdom, the
proleptic anticipation of its contours and structures of non-

violent communication in love and service to widows, orphans, the poor, the stranger in the land, the neighbor.

Without in any way endorsing the entirety of Moltmann's theological construal, I would contend that it is undeniable, as John Howard Yoder argues in his *The Politics of Jesus*, that discipleship to Jesus entails a principled commitment to nonviolence. Yoder sums up the main elements in an ethics of discipleship: a critique of power, a sense of the meaning of suffering, a search for authenticity, a visible and voluntary community, a universal vision.[23] In Yoder's view, the primary category for grounding an ethics of discipleship is less rational deliberation and public discourse about "secular warrants" than obedience. This ethics of discipleship becomes "public" in and through the church, which functions as a particular community of discernment (with an education toward discerning discipleship in a "secret discipline" of prayer, ethics, and service). It serves as well as a contrasting model to the state or merely secular notions of citizenship. In the final analysis, in Christian ethics we are called to be saints and not merely citizens.

Sobrino contends that the directionality of an ethics of discipleship can be found in the Old Testament ideals of covenant and kingdom: care for widows, orphans, the stranger in the land, the poor; and in the New Testament ideal of neighbor love (expressed strongly in the parable of the good Samaritan [Luke 10:25–37] and the last judgment in Matthew 25) where each person in need—even the stranger or the enemy—becomes the neighbor. Unlike Yoder, Sobrino postulates that an ethics of discipleship can serve as a rightful criterion not only to judge from outside but also to transform political action. The rights of the poor, as the early church writers expressed, become the criterion for right government.[24] Critics have assumed that an ethics of discipleship perforce lacks explicit political intent because it is primarily personalistic or individualistic—in my eyes, a gross misreading of the communal thrust of biblical thought. Others see it as, at best, an exclusively ecclesial ethic. As they judge, in biblical times Christians were never concerned directly with social structures, which they simply took for granted. Responding to this objection, Edward Schillebeeckx has argued that the New Testament does not ignore social structures but tended, for historical reasons based on expectations of the imminent second coming and the limited access to societal power, to build alternative structures alongside, rather than within, Roman society. Early Christianity conceived these structures of the church, however, not as pure "eschatological witness," but as the concrete embodiment and model for *any* genuinely righteous society, wherever it was found. Schillebeeckx contends that it is difficult to construct a consistent ethic of two separate kingdoms (in Luther's sense) on this biblical vision.[25]

In the New Testament view, the best that can be said for state power and citizenship is that, although they are merely provisional, they can be used as an instrument for God's righteous purposes. Alternately, they represent the embodiment of anti-god and injustice. There is no exalted or developed notion of citizenship in the New Testament material. On the other hand, it seems clear that the New Testament does not restrict metanoia (deep conversion) to purely inward personal conversion, nor does it see church life as a merely separate eschatological enclave with no relevance for societal life. There is little evidence that early Christians failed to use the ethics of discipleship as a measure for judging secular citizenship; their ethics served as its judge, model, and, ideally, if the situation was ripe, its tutor. In this sense, an ethics of discipleship includes a political intent. On that point Yoder's *The Politics of Jesus* is convincingly persuasive.

Yet even struggling saints must know that no state, short of the reign of Christ, will embody the structures of the reign of God. This realization led Reinhold Niebuhr to describe the ethics of discipleship as an "impossible ideal." Niebuhr contended that it is both necessary and possible to make discriminating judgments among competing contenders for worldly citizenship and rough justice here below. Hence Niebuhr rightly argued for the need for some independent notion of citizenship and justice in a society not populated by saints and heroes. Niebuhr, however, continued to hope for a paradoxical and dialectical tensive correlation between discipleship and citizenship.[26] We need, then, to consider now the meaning of citizenship.

3. The Meaning of Citizenship

Ours remains a decidedly pluralistic political world. We need to distinguish, then, widely divergent groundings for the moral ideal of citizenship. Michael Walzer in his "The Concept of Citizenship" postulates three quite different foundations of citizenship. Walzer rejects a purely passive-servile notion by which citizens are duty-bound to civic obligations because they are recipients of benefits only the state can provide. As Walzer notes, we are fundamentally citizens because of our membership in a determined society that precedes and dictates, to a large extent, the form of the polity. Society precedes the state. Walzer argues that the citizen is not primarily bound to the state authorities at all but to other citizens. In this view, Walzer rejects a Hobbesian or even the more benign Lockean concept of a social contract. Walzer roots his notion of citizenship implicitly in some idea of a common good greater than particular interest and civic benevolence as members of a common historic people. Citizenship rights, at base, are membership rights in a historic community. Walzer also argues that passive-servile concepts of citizenship yield little protection against despotic majority rule or the tyrannical state. We do not do well to hypothesize a Leviathan State or some abstract "general will."

Although Walzer finds the unmediated active democratic citizenship of the Athenian polis a congenial model, he notes that, in modern complex societies, the citizen will lack both sufficient time and expertise to direct administration effectively or to determine the common good to a particular enactment in law that foresees and regulates fairly wider societal consequences, trade-offs, and political possibilities. In the earlier Athenian ideal of citizenship, citizens obeyed the laws, since they were an expression of their own active agency and will. Walzer opts for a pluralist notion of citizenship carried by associations active in the common interest. This notion is akin to Athenian citizenship but recognizes the impossibility of face-to-face direct democracy. The associations active in the common interest that Walzer has in mind are different from pure single-issue political action committees. They look to the common rather than to the particular interest. Walzer envisions something other than a citizenship based on a neutral state regulating plea bargaining between purely private interests. He assumes that a modern, active, and critical citizenship will entail some expenditure, beyond mere suffrage, of the citizen's time, money, and personal engagement in setting policy and the terms for public argument. Membership in associations concerned with the public welfare mediates the active Athenian role of citizen-politicians.

Walzer comments that, in this present age of media politics and primary elections as beauty contests, "voting is lifted out of the context of parties and platforms; it is more like impulse buying than political decision making." In contrast, Walzer sets out the ideal of an active democratic citizenship where "every citizen is a potential participant, a potential politician."[27] Unlike discipleship, which is an exclusionary concept, citizenship points to an inclusive membership category. Walzer remarks to this effect that "it is only as members somewhere that men and women can hope to share in all the other social goods—security, wealth, honor, office and power—that communal life makes possible."[28]

Whoever genuinely participates in the economy and law of a society, Walzer argues, should be regarded (and ought to be able to regard themselves) as potential or future participants in politics as well. He rejects any notion of a semipermanent alien category such as the guest-worker class in European nations. All members of society enjoy a range of citizen rights and duties in respect to security, welfare, and equality of access to public office and to the basic equal education of citizens. Citizens must enjoy equal rights to exercise minimal political power (voting rights) and to try to exercise greater power (speech, assembly, and petition rights).

As I have already noted, Walzer exhibits ambiguity about any substantive notion of justice. Indeed, he assumes that the root meaning of equality is negative, the freedom from extrinsic domination. He eschews any appeals to anthropological constants in the *humanum*. His is a pluralist, procedural notion of distributive justice based on the concept of complex equality where "different social goods ought to be distributed for different reasons, in accordance with different procedures, by different agents."[29] Walzer is also a social relativist. "All distributions are just or unjust relative to the social meanings of the goods at stake."[30] Social meanings, in turn, are radically historical, changing over time. As he states it, "Every substantive account of distributive justice is a local account."[31] Some empirical overlap may occur in a conception of social goods across human societies. This overlap, however, allows no legitimate philosophical generalizations as in a species of natural law or natural rights.

Walzer's genuinely rich notion of differentiated spheres of justice, as we have seen, entails a strong separation of citizenship and discipleship. Rough justice envisions a citizenry vitally concerned with monitoring the boundaries between the differentiated spheres of property, work, love, religion, politics, and status. Walzer's scheme leaves little room for an integrating vision of society above (and, presumably, respectful of) the differentiated spheres of justice. Like Ricoeur, Walzer sees keenly the essential ambiguity of state power:

> It is the crucial agency of distributive justice; it guards the boundaries within which every social good is distributed and deployed. Hence the simultaneous requirements that power be sustained and that it be inhibited: mobilized, divided, checked and balanced. Political power protects us from tyranny . . . and itself becomes tyrannical. And it is for both these reasons that power is so much desired and so endlessly fought over.[32]

If, as Walzer argues, good fences make for good justice and good neighbors, he leaves little room for a concept of citizenship that might at least approximate that neighbor love which is the key to any correlation between discipleship and citizenship.

In Walzer's understanding, vital democratic citizenship depends on a differentiated conception of social goods. Democracy is less a tradition of substantive justice than a sustained, procedurally fair argument about policy among those with, presumably, radically divergent substantive visions of virtue, justice, the integrated life, and the social good. Efficiency in arguing one's case (whether the argument is true or not) and voting function as the only legitimate ways to distribute and judge political power. Although, in one place only, Walzer speaks of "citizenly virtue," his conception of virtue is curiously vacuous. He lacks the Aristotelian notion of public education as character formation in a polis to produce the type of virtuous activity essential to sustain a determined state constitution. Justice is a culturally relative term, "rooted in the distinct understandings of places, honors, jobs, things of all sorts, that constitute a shared way of life."[33] Thus, in the end, Walzer's argument for citizen justice in our own society is, primarily, a story of societal and procedural arrangements:

> a decentralized democratic socialism; a strong welfare state run, in part at least, by local and amateur officials; a constrained market; an open and demystified civil service; independent public schools; the sharing of hard work and free time; the protection of religions and familial life; a system of public honoring and dishonoring free from all considerations of rank or class; workers' control of companies and factories; a politics of parties, movements, meetings and public debate.[34]

Eternal vigilance, guaranteed through an education for citizenship, is the price we must pay for both liberty and complex equality. The vigilance looks to transgressions of the boundaries between spheres of justice. It lacks any substantive vision of the good and the integrated life.

Despite Waltzer's disclaimers to any substantive anthropology or "natural law," I do not think that his attractive conception of an active and vigilant citizenship can ultimately be sustained on his culturally relativistic grounds. In the absence of a more substantive anthropology, Walzer ends up espousing what Bellah and his colleagues in *Habits of the Heart* call a "politics of interest," where "politics means the pursuit of differing interests according to agreed-upon, neutral rules."[35] Bellah and his associates contrast this purely procedural notion of citizenship with two other concepts of politics: (1) the politics of making operative the moral consensus of the community reached through free face-to-face discussion and (2) a politics of the nation expressed in the language of national purpose.[36]

Bellah and his associates root their more substantive concept of citizenship in a deep sense of a certain kind of human character. They postulate that justice is the guiding end of citizenship.[37] Like Walzer, they see that citizenship is a cooperative form of life wherein "the individual self finds its fulfillment in relationships with others in a society, organized through public dialogue."[38] *Habits of the Heart* argues, however, to a notion of the self sustained only by practices within communities of memory that engender habits of substantive commitments and virtue. In the end, a socially unanchored self lacks any meaning, larger purpose, or a narrative framework to make sense of suffering, death, the struggle for justice, love and commitment, and citizenship itself. Against cultural relativism, *Habits of the Heart* argues that, perhaps, "there are practices of life, good in themselves, that are inherently fulfilling."[39] Its authors can speak—in categories that break the differentiated spheres whose fenced-off boundaries are so crucial to Walzer—of citizenship as "civic friendship" and indispensable social practices that are "ethically good in themselves."[40]

Concerning the contribution of religion to citizenship, Walzer attempts, primarily, in a negative injunction, to keep the religious sphere from influencing or contaminating the notion of citizenship. Bellah and his associates, on the other hand, assume, following Alexis de Tocqueville, that religion remains the first of our political institutions. Religion has political impact not because it directly intervenes in politics—this is avoided through our constitutional separation of church and state—but as supportive of those mores which alone anchor a republic and make democracy possible. To allow the state a monopoly in forming national character would be to court tyranny. The church, institutionally set off from direct intrusions in politics or the intervention of the state in its sphere, is not separated from *society*. Unless the religious community can maintain itself as a vigorous community of memory, it will have little to add to citizenship. The authors of *Habits of the Heart* see keenly that citizenship will degenerate into an empty category in the absence of vigorous religious communities of memory. This argument is central in classic political thought: without virtuous citizens, no republic can withstand tyranny; without vital religion, no virtuous citizenry.

Walzer and Bellah and his associates remind us that the notion of politics and citizens contains positive elements concerned, at the least, with the secular human minimum, a Platonic shadow of what Christians would call justice, human dignity, a flourishing diversity mirroring the polyvalent God. In its highest forms the civic republican tradition (partly itself shaped under Christian influence) embraces something akin to compassionate neighbor love, a redemptive suffering service, communal enlargement, and sustaining commitments in practices of the good. Christians are not well served to bring *only* suspicions to the notion of citizenship. If all secular notions of citizenship fall far short of discipleship to the way of Jesus, some bear at least a faint analogical resemblance to the high notion of discipleship. Such notions offer a point of contact for correlation between the two ethics.

Neither Walzer nor the authors of *Habits of the Heart* are blind to the temptations of politics to foster cupidity, narrowness of spirit, greed, and dominative power. On their part, Bellah and his associates come close to invoking the Christian language of sin to describe political corruption or narrow individualistic narcissisms. Yet neither Walzer nor Bellah and his associates, in my view, in their highlighting of the ways in which political power can further rationality and justice, pay sufficient heed to the intrinsic paradox of state political power as involving, *inextricably* interwoven, both rationality and violence. *Habits of the Heart* seems to give complete equal weight to discipleship and civic republican virtue in ways that miss the Christian correlation of the two from the starting point of discipleship as the *determining* partner in the dialogue. Still, *Habits of the Heart* serves important notice to Christians that, in a culture dominated by what its authors refer to as "utilitarian" and "expressive" individualism, Christians find it very difficult to speak their own appropriate language of discipleship. This would seem to me to point to the urgent need for fostering a distinctively Christian pedagogy of discipleship that approaches its bilingual conversation with citizenship in clear command of its own vocabulary. If I understand correctly the argument of *Habits of the Heart*, Christians will not educate successfully for citizenship for a better and more just world unless they first induct members of the churches into a vigorous community of memory whose special and particular memory is that of disciples who follow the practices of Jesus.

4. Neighbor and Social Companion: Citizenship and Discipleship as Interrelated

Violence is the decisive factor that grounds the distinction between citizenship, even at its best, and discipleship. Discipleship, in principle, looks to the enactment of the utopian, nonviolent reign of God, an arena of undistorted communication without domination (to use Jürgen Habermas's categories), founded in neighbor love. Citizenship grows out of membership in a community whose political authority necessarily rests, at crucial points, in coercion and, at times, domination. When necessary, the state claims the right to resort to violence. This element of violence, however, is never or rarely pure. Rather, as Paul Ricoeur has noted, "the state is a great mystery. The state represents an unresolved contradiction, lying always midway between rationality and coercion."[41] Thus, as Ricoeur goes on to state, "There is no such thing as a Christian politics, only the politics of Christians who are also citizens."[42]

Yet, in the actual empirical functioning of church and state, it would be a serious mistake to draw sharp divisions between the two realms as empirical realities. Edward Schillebeeckx alerts us to the danger of any easy "good guy-bad guy" images. "We should also realize that precisely because the religious is always a dimension of the total culture, every religion (Christianity included) inevitably has both liberating *and* alienating effects."[43]

Citizenship and discipleship, while distinct, are also closely interrelated. As I noted, a strong tradition in political thought maintains that religion fulfills an indispensable role in character formation in society, the development of citizens who embody specific virtues, discipline, purpose, and commitment to communal solidarity beyond self-interest. Just this indispensable civic role of religion in instilling habits of the heart and character traits *(les moeurs)* essential for the survival of a republic prompted Alexis de Tocqueville to see it as the first of America's political institutions.

Ricoeur and Schillebeeckx can help us see why disciples will also concern themselves with citizenship. Both authors rely on a sense of the social and of culture as mediating the *humanum* for Christian anthropology. Both rely essentially on a theology of creation. God loves the created order and the creaturely human which coshapes every human order and invests it with human purposes. Relying on this strong social sense, Ricoeur comments, "Every access to the human condition depends on and presupposes access to citizenship, and citizens, in their turn, come to their citizenship through membership in the state."[44]

Schillebeeckx evokes the great symbol of the human as *imago Dei*, the one permissible image of God that is not an idolatry. Noting that the book of Revelation represents a permanent resource for a Christian liberation theology and for Christian hope for the struggle for justice in a history that might be best described as "an oecumene of suffering," Schillebeeckx argues that the central image of God presented in Revelation is of the one who champions every good and fights every evil.

> For the believer, the *humanum*, in this world, represents the foundational symbol of the holy, of God as the champion of every good and the challenger of every evil. Humanity, then, in the arena where that struggle against good and evil actually takes place, represents a potent revelation of God as grace and judgment.[45]

While no actual politics is totally pure or free from the corruption of coercion and violence, politics represents a privileged arena where the argument and struggle between good and evil occurs in concrete terms and around determinate policies and legislation. Politics in the broad sense (not just that waged by political parties but also that carried by social and cultural movements) represents the place for discernment of emerging good and evil in history. Few can doubt the centrality of the political for good and evil. For political power, as Walzer tells us, regulates every social good. The concrete face and fate of the *humanum* is being determined every day in political struggle and concurring agreements that reach toward consensus. Destinations and human risks are what politics is about, and power is the ability to settle these questions. As Walzer puts it, "Politics is always the most direct path to dominance, and political power (rather than the means of production) is probably the most important, and certainly the most dangerous, good in human history. . . . However it is had and whoever has it, power is the regulative agency for social goods generally."[46]

It should be obvious, then, why the church in its education for discipleship cannot ignore citizenship. The tangible and accessible image of God, the *humanum*, and the very concrete, culturally mediated struggle for the good and fight against evil take place in the everyday arena of citizenship and politics. Ricoeur details the ways in which neighbor love gets embodied through social institutions and the texture of social roles. He notes that, at times, even the appropriate object of neighbor love is revealed to us only when we see our neighbors in and through their collective social existence and vast collective ills and suffering: race discrimination, unemployment, colonial and neo-colonial domination, systematic genocide and torture. Political and social structures often seem abstractions. Yet the abstract protects and nurtures the concrete. Only healthy social conditions, even if they seem far removed from the intimacy of concrete, interpersonal encounter, allow for a genuine continuing intimacy.[47]

Ricoeur invokes the minority status of Christians in the world and notes that "the world" is a biblical symbol as the eschatological horizon of salvation, liberation in Christ and grace in history. Ricoeur argues for a direct preaching to the world that does not take place just in and through the church. "If the church has any good news for the world concerning the political problems of our world, then, in a certain sense [its] religious message needs to be preached over the heads of believers to the world as such."[48]

In summary, I propose my *second thesis* concerning discipleship and citizenship: the *church that educates for discipleship must also educate for citizenship.*

The Synod of Roman Catholic Bishops meeting in Rome in 1971 prepared a document entitled "Justice in the World" which strongly supports this thesis. These bishops caught in their pronouncements the important nexus between discipleship and citizenship: "Action on behalf of justice and participation in the transformation of the world fully appear to us as a constitutive dimension of preaching the gospel or, in other words, of the church's mission for the redemption of the human race and its liberation from every oppressive structure."[49] The Synod went on to say, "The mission of preaching the gospel dictates . . . that we dedicate ourselves to the liberation of humans even in their present existence. . . . For unless the Christian message of love and justice shows its effectiveness through action in the world, it will only with difficulty gain credibility in our times."[50]

A similar note can be heard in the stirring documents from the bishops of Latin America at their General Conferences at Medellin (1968) and Puebla (1979) and in recent papal pronouncements. Representative are the balanced remarks of Pope Paul VI in a general audience not long before his death: "There is no doubt that everything which touches human promotion, that is, the work for justice, development and peace in all parts of the world ought also to be an integral part of the message [of the gospel]. . . . Do not separate human liberation and salvation in Jesus, *without however identifying them.*"[51]

5. What Citizenship Adds to Discipleship

The Christian doctrines of creation and incarnation subsume a belief about an intrinsic relation between God and the world, between God and humanity. Christians believe that God is in the world and that the world is with God, yet they in no way reduce God to the world or the world to God. Christians claim that no area of life, in principle, falls outside the reach of the gracious action of God. Hence, Christians cannot maintain that politics can be totally isolated or separated from the religious sphere of life.

Nevertheless, as we have seen, Christians have no privileged access to social-political questions, no special blueprint for the economic and social order, no substitute access to political technique and the density of political experience which comes only from sustained engagement in political movements.[52] As we saw Ricoeur put it, there is no specifically Christian politics. As a result, a specifically Christian political party involves a dangerous strategy. It may be a pretentious illusion, in principle

even a contradiction of terms.[53] Christians must wager their
political bets and conduct political strategy simply in their capacity as citizens. As Christian "materialists" in their response to
the incarnation and creation, they must respect the integrity and
opacity of the "material" of political forces, constraints, and
historical possibilities that comprises every determinate social
order.

I would propose that citizenship adds three qualities to discipleship. First, it *widens the reach of Christian solidarity* to include all
other citizens in its range, thereby reminding Christians that
God's grace reigns outside church borders. This wider solidarity
shown by Christian concern and co-stewardship with fellow
citizens for the political keeps vividly alive the important ecclesial truth that Christian preaching and witness, indeed the
church itself, exist *for* the world. "The world" serves as an eschatological symbol of the church's mission which must extend
to all times, places, peoples, and spheres of life, "even to the
ends of the earth." The duties of citizenship protect the church
from narrow parochial introspection. They provide a deeper
sense of mission and of the scope of neighbor love. Finally,
solidarity as citizen-disciples can focus the Christian worship of
God on God's only accessible image, the *humanum*.

A second note that citizenship adds to discipleship is *a humbler
service* in the often intractable day-to-day reality of politics. By
recognizing the arena of politics as a field of contradiction between rationality and justice, power and violence, the goal of
this Christian service in the political arena will be, in the words
of Ricoeur, "simultaneously to improve the political institutions
in the sense of the achievement of greater rationality and to
remain wary of the abuse of power that is ingredient in every
state system."[54] Ultimately, the temptation to abuse of power
can be undercut only by dividing power. Power, in turn, can be
divided only if it is controlled and kept on a human scale.
Christians claim to carry a special vision of what constitutes the
humanum, to be, in Pope Paul VI's fine phrase in his address to
the United Nations, "experts in humanity." They disclaim any
special expertise in the techniques, use, and creativity ingredient in political power. Through a common struggle with other

citizens to tame and channel power to creative use in the service of their guiding vision of the human, they learn the humble way of shared responsibility and solidarity in history.

Finally, the political represents *a taxing reality test*, an experiential proving ground for Christian claims for a this-worldly, liberative, regenerative potential in grace and redemption. As Schillebeeckx forcefully argues, the central Christian truth claims remain also experiential concepts, subject to evidential test in praxis and history.[55] Hence, the taxing reality test of discipleship in citizenship is not a luxury on Christian grounds. In and through this reality test, Christians put flesh on their hopes for a transformed future based on the already achieved and transforming power of Christ in history. This is an evidential claim.

In the political order, human beings dissect reality, discern countertrends and movements, and touch their deepest desires for a more human community and future. If a cleavage between discipleship and citizenship, between Max Weber's ethics of absolute ends and ethics of responsibility, remains until the end times, there can be moments when, asymptotically, they approach a genuine correlation. The German Lutheran martyr Dietrich Bonhoeffer caught this truth when he argued that Christians must risk what he calls a civic "venture of responsibility" in which they act, as Christians, on behalf of those without power, using whatever power they have for the protection of the powerless. Robin Lovin describes the meaning of this citizen venture of responsibility: "The specifically Christian marks of obedience are largely absent from the venture of responsibility. It is an act based on a sound reading of the facts and a type of civil courage which can and must be shared with others; and yet, properly understood, the venture involves a risk of personal corruption. . . . Only one who believes in the power of Christian grace is likely to undertake it."[56]

Discipleship—rendering present, at least in fragmented anticipations, the reign of God—depends on what Christians call "reading the signs of the times." One cannot discern the signs of the times—what Paul Lehmann refers to as "finding out what God is doing in history"—without simultaneously venturing the risk of fully entering, with fellow citizens, the times whose shape, promise, and future direction will largely depend on what citizens do together within their political order.

6. What Discipleship Adds to Citizenship

In a recent book on Christian faith and social criticism, the Flemish Jesuit scholar Louis van Bladel suggests the triad: (1) the gospel as promise: utopia; (2) the gospel as judgment: counter-culture; and (3) the gospel as vocation: the construction of a new order.[57] I wish to draw upon van Bladel in developing my third thesis, namely, that a Christian citizen's duties are greater and different from a citizen's duties as the state understands them. Specifically, I want to propose that the special contribution of discipleship to citizenship can be found in these three notes: *utopia, counterculture,* and *vocation.*

We have come to recognize the crucial importance of utopian vision for politics. It breaks the stranglehold of currently reigning paradigms, frees our imaginations to consider alternatives, and functions against every determinism to remind us that politics is a human game, the product, ultimately, of human choices and the limitations of human hopes and dreams. We ourselves construct the social world which in turn constrains us and hems us in. Van Bladel suggests the power of symbols of healing, forgiveness, and integrity to unleash new moments of political imagination. The impossible, outside the range of the art of the politically imaginable, nonetheless suddenly becomes possible. The previously unimaginable and unthinkable captures, at certain moments in history, the minds and hearts of citizens. So began the civil rights movement, the abolition of slavery, the rise of labor unions, feminist struggles for suffrage, and equal opportunities in our American social history.

Ricoeur, on his part, notes that this utopian imagination diminishes the chasm between the violent pedagogy of the state based on power and force and the nonviolent pedagogy of neighbor love. Paradoxically, he comments, at times, the non-violent resister steps outside the range of legally authorized behavior and, in so doing, calls the state back to its true vocation by reminding it that it only exists to bring human beings to freedom, equality, and conditions of dignity. The nonviolence of nuclear pacifists, movements of Franciscan poverty, the Greens (an ecological movement in Germany, Holland, and Belgium), and ecologists serve notice that the state exists for the welfare of human beings, and not vice versa. In a fine phrase, Ricoeur evokes a "salvation through imaginative power." He comments: "Every conversion, in the first instance, involves a revolution in the images that guide our lives. By changing their self-image, human beings change their existence."[58] Every revolution in history has begun with a call for new patterns of human interaction. Ordinary politics, by focusing on the presently possible, tends to deaden or narrow our political imaginations. Disciple-citizens, taking inspiration from the gospel utopia, can keep that imagination open.

The gospel also "convicts of sin." Van Bladel draws on a rich set of social science resources (Karl Marx, Herbert Marcuse, Jean Baudrillard, René Girard) to map the social-structural terrain where we are politically and culturally unfree, unjust, and lacking in hope and love in our modern, technico-rational consumer societies. Appealing to the New Testament stress on the battle against "the powers" which dominate and suffocate human beings, van Bladel combines evangelical inspiration with the social-critical thought of the human sciences to outline what gospel judgment might mean in advanced, technical societies.[59] In van Bladel's view, Christians are called to be countercultural to everything in our society that stands for death, unfreedom, and injustice.

Finally, Christians view their life as a vocation, a calling to construct—using the only political materials we human beings have at hand—at least an approximation of that undistorted communication in neighbor love envisioned by God's new community. Hence, for van Bladel, beyond critical negativity, beyond eschatological reserve against every historical social achievement, and beyond countercultural refusals discipleship must also unleash the constructive power of vocation to build, in and through the present structures, a more habitable commonwealth through what Bonhoeffer called the "venture of responsibility."

In several places in his political writings, Ricoeur echoes these same themes of utopia, counterculture, and constructive vocation. Against the dangers of power, he poses the Christian nonviolent counterpoise; against the temptation to greed or the alienation of commodity fetishism in possession and property, he suggests Franciscan movements of simplicity and the Calvinist sense of careful stewardship of earthly goods which really belong to all; against culturally restricted values he proposes catholicity, keeping alive a human project that envisions a global unity transcending national boundaries. It is not that Christians have any pat answers. Rather, the task of the Christian in politics, according to Ricoeur, is "so to act that in society the issues of the use and meaning of power, the pleasure principle and human autonomy as a value can be brought at least, once again, into serious public discussion."[60]

In discussing the interconnection and tension between neighbor and social companion, Ricoeur shows the peculiar relevance of discipleship to citizenship:

> The theme of neighbor-love contains a permanent criticism on larger social bonds and inter-actions: according to the measure of neighbor-love, the larger social nexus is never intimate enough and never sufficiently inclusive. Social structures are never intimate enough because structurally mediated social inter-actions can never be the equivalent of an unmediated presence and meeting in personal dialogue. They are never inclusive enough since social groups can only achieve their distinct identity by contrasting themselves to out-groups. Hence, they fall back into self-enclosure in their own enclave. Christian neighbor-love involves the double demand of being simultaneously close and far away. The Samaritan represents being close because he came close-by and yet he represents being far-away because as a non-Jew, on a given day, he stayed with an unknown stranger who had been attacked by the wayside.[61]

Thus, neighbor love functions to bridge the chasm between citizenship and discipleship by serving as a permanent reminder that the ultimate purpose of any politics and citizenship is the service that political structures render to concrete human beings in their material and spiritual needs. Ricoeur concludes his reflections with the remark, "What the final judgment implies, it seems to me, is that we will be judged by what we did in very abstract institutional settings and structures to make them serve neighbor-love, often without being personally conscious of how our actions in these social structures actually impacted on the lives of the individual human beings touched by them."[62]

7. Some Central New Testament Texts on Citizenship and Ethics

It will not be possible to develop, at any length, an expanded exegesis of the set of New Testament texts that treat the topic of citizenship. Despite its importance as a permanent counterweight to Romans 13, I will leave aside the teaching of Revelation 13 (and elsewhere), which represents a powerful religious critique of the absolute, arbitrary, imperial power that the book of Relevation sees as an embodiment of Satan. Against the Roman cry of "Imperator Victor," it is Jesus who is proclaimed "Victor" in the struggle. "He has overcome" (Revelation 5:5). Nor will I deal with the important and nuanced theory of civic obedience in 1 Peter with its insistence that the state is a mere human creation (*ktisis;* cf. 1 Peter 2:13). 1 Peter suggests that the imperial power often acts as an antichrist (cf. 1 Peter 3:14–17; 4:12–19; 5:13). Yet 1 Peter calls for a free obedience to the state authorities (1 Peter 2:16), in hopes that the good behavior of Christians will clear up misunderstandings (including the misunderstandings after 66 C.E. that early Christians might be connected with the Palestinian Jewish revolutionaries) and reduce injustice. In contrast to Romans 13:7, which calls upon Christians to show a "reverential fear" for both God and emperor, carelessly using the same religious term, *phobein,* for both, 1 Peter 2:17 uses two different words, thus enjoining two quite specifically different acts: "Reverence God with fear and respect the emperor" *(ton theon phobeisthe, ton basilea timate).* Everywhere the New Testament rejects any Christian participation in the imperial cult.

Mark 12:13–17, concerning coin tribute to Caesar, and Romans 13:1–7 need special comment and exegesis because of their frequent use and misuse as a common proof texts concerning discipleship and citizenship. Many have, mistakenly, considered the famous proverb, "Pay to Caesar the tax that is due him and give to God what belongs to God," as settling, in one fine formula, the permanent demarcations between religion and politics. The literary genre of Mark 12:13–17 is that of a contestation-debate saying between Jesus and his enemies. Throughout Mark 12 the deadly conflict between Jesus and certain Jewish leaders unfolds; the high priests, scribes, and elders (Mark 11:27), the Pharisees and the Herodians (Mark 12:13), the Sadducees (Mark 12:18), and finally again the scribes (Mark 12:28), though, as in all the Gospel accounts, these texts are layered with the later conflicts between Jewish leadership and Christians in the final third of the first century.

Mark is absolutely uninterested in providing information about Jesus' own position on the state, as his use of the genre contestation-debate shows in this pericope. Whatever that position may have been lies outside Mark's intention in Chapter 12. Rather, the narrative relates how, when some of his fellow Jews, in positions of authority, pose a trick question, Jesus sees through it. He counters with a question that foils their attempts to pin him down. Jesus asks them whose image is on the coin of the realm. The authorities produce a coin, already a sign that they themselves stand within the Roman system as a de facto reality. Jesus produces no coin himself. Jesus plays with their foil by trapping them within the framework of their own question. "Since you yourselves already obviously stand within the system, well, then, pay your taxes [the technical meaning of *apodidonai*] to Caesar and give God what is God's due."

That this is a contestation saying is clear from the finale in Mark 12:17: "And they remained amazed at him." Jesus successfully avoided the trap set for him without having really to commit himself on the question by which, whichever way he answered, he would be compromised. As Schillebeeckx notes, "The literary genre of the contestation-saying does not allow us to see Mark 12:13–17 as a teaching-saying of Jesus (which follows another literary genre) concerning faith and politics."[63] The exegetical misreading of Mark 12:13–17 by taking this contestation saying out of its appropriate context and absolutizing it as a principle of Christians in politics is not valid. Moreover, the usual interpretation of the saying as postulating a rigid cleavage between the social-political and religious is foreign both to Mark and to the whole of the New Testament. As Matthew's Gospel states in a genuine teaching saying: one cannot serve two masters, God and mammon (Matthew 6:24; cf. Luke 16:13). For the Christian the world of politics and money must also be seen in relation to God. This means that the Christian must also be seen as facing *religious* decisions on these issues too.

If it is impossible to find in Mark 12:13–17 any indication of early Christianity's attitude toward the duties of citizenship, Romans 13:1–7 serves as the primary text enjoining civic obedience. This text, too, suffers from frequent reading out of context. We need to pay attention to several factors crucial to understanding the Pauline text. No doubt there existed among certain New Testament writers an apologetic concern to downplay any sense of Christian disloyalty to the state or any Christian connection with Jewish zealot revolutionaries after about 66 C.E. Paul, particularly, would be favorably disposed toward Rome as both a Roman citizen and as a diaspora Jew. The latter status, especially, determines the meaning of Romans 13. From the time of the diaspora, Judaism faced the need to distinguish the political state from the believing community. Diaspora Judaism showed a certain benevolence toward heathen political power. Thus Deutero-Isaiah could refer to the Persian king as "anointed of God" (Isaiah 45:1) and even see Cyrus as "servant" of God's will. In this view, political power could serve as an instrument of God's purposes, but its religious weight was only in terms of what it could do *in respect to the community of Israel.* Absolutely no religious significance was accorded to political sovereignty in its own right.

It is important to note that Paul neglects any directly christological allusions in Romans 13. He simply takes over the position of diaspora Judaism and repeats it for the church. Thus Romans 13:4 can speak of the Roman authority, like Cyrus, as God's servant *(diakonos).* But there is no distinctively Christian element in the entire pericope. Paul's advice to the early Christian community in Rome is simply that it should follow the Jewish model. The community follows its own church order in internal relations (cf. 1 Corinthians 5—6). An internally organized religious community, the diaspora Jewish rule, in respect to pagan civil authority, holds (1) an attitude of civil loyalty, (2) passive but stubborn resistance to any religious persecution; and (3) a positive enactment of ordinary civil duties (e.g., taxes).

Christians seek no special privileges in the pagan state, as a result of their belief. They share the same civil duties as any other citizens, although they deny any sacral significance to the state as such. Indeed, civil duties as such involve an ethical, not a religious, question (cf. Romans 13:5, "It is necessary to obey . . . *as a matter of conscience*" [emphasis added]). Citizenship is an issue of ethical, not specifically Christian, duty. The genuine Christian duty enunciated by Paul surpasses citizenship: have love for the other, since the one who loves the neighbor fulfills the whole law (Romans 13:8–10). Romans 13:8–10 is a necessary context for a correct reading of vv. 1–7, as is 12:9–21, which precedes the pericope, containing the great Pauline hymn to love and the appended virtues of self-sacrificing neighbor love. The full context of Romans 13:1–7, then, suggests that in the question of duties of citizenship, Christians have the same duties as other citizens. Citizenship as such has no sacral meaning. It belongs purely to the realm of ethics, a matter of conscience (Romans 13:6).

But on either side of the Romans 13 pericope lies the greater and different duty of Christians in their worldly life: a neighbor love that surpasses what mere civil law can enact or demand. Since Christians find themselves in a situation similar to diaspora Judaism, they should seek the benevolence of the authorities which, quite unwittingly, may be used by God, as Cyrus was for the exiles in Babylon, for the benefit of Christians. In this narrow sense, civil authority is from the hand of God (as indeed all authority falls under God's supreme authority).

The background of diaspora Judaism as a key to understanding Romans 13 becomes much clearer if we juxtapose it with the other Pauline saying on civil authority (1 Timothy 2:1–15) which enjoins Christian prayer for the authorities (as diaspora Judaism prayed), "so that we might be able to live an undisturbed life in peace, with piety and uprightness." In sum, the proper reading of the teaching of Romans 13:1–10 (putting vv. 1–7 in its fuller context) is as follows:

> As citizens you should faithfully fulfill the ordinary civil duties as a matter of conscience. As Christians, of course, you are bound to much more: genuine love for the other modeled on God's covenant

love. Fulfill your civil duties in the context of your discipleship, as a portion of this wider neighbor love which forms the necessary context for understanding citizenship.[64]

This exegesis of Romans 13 raises the larger question about a distinctive Christian ethic for worldly behavior. It would take us too far afield to defend, fully, the position I want to argue here. Thus I will merely state my position and draw its implications for the issue of correlating discipleship and citizenship.

In general, I want to maintain that the New Testament ethic is a transformative ethic which always presupposes another given, underlying societal ethic as the material on which it works the Christian transformation. Although almost half of the Pauline material consists of ethical casuistry or teaching, I would argue that the general pattern followed in the New Testament is the pattern found in the Pauline *Haustafeln* (see Colossians 3:18—4:1; Ephesians 5:22—6:9; 1 Timothy 2:1–15; 6:1–2; Titus 2:1–10; 1 Peter 2:13—3:9). My thesis is that all directly normative material in the New Testament is taken over from earlier Jewish or Roman-Greek stoic material (none of which, except for the religious basis of Jewish ethics in the Old Testament, has a religious ground). Thus there are no specifically Christian norms besides the cultural norms of the societies within which Christianity lived (and now lives). In the New Testament, Christians are urged to live moral lives in accord with the highest available societal ethical codes. Rather than a separate sets of norms, Christians are urged to live and transform the available ethos of their societies, "in the Lord" (cf. Ephesians 5:22–33; 1 Peter 2:13–14). Discipleship, as we have seen, is primarily an ethics of following the pattern of Jesus' dispositions, paradigmatic actions, and utopian teachings in the new, different context in which we live, not a slavish reconstruction of the context (and underlying ethos) of early Palestinian Jewish society or the Hellenistic world.

In that sense, as Schillebeeckx argues, "the New Testament was always searching for the appropriate correlation between salvation in Christ and ethics."[65] The key to this correlation is found in having the attitude of self-sacrifice and love, "the same attitude as Jesus had" (Phil. 2:5). With that attitude the first

Christians were urged by the New Testament to internalize the best of the received Jewish or, in gentile Christianity, Hellenic Stoic cultural ethos and enact it, "in the Lord." After all, as a new sect, early Christianity had no cultural ethos of its own.

If my thesis here has merit, it would suggest another motive for the correlation of discipleship and citizenship. Christians claim no transcultural, normative ethos of their own unrelated to or in permanent tension with the citizenly ethos of their host societies. Rather, they internalize and enact the set of virtues necessary for a good society in their host cultures and live them, in a transformative manner, as disciples, "in the Lord." In that sense, like the Christians of the New Testament, today's Christians are always seeking the appropriate relationship between discipleship and citizenship. No pat formula solves this relationship once and for all. It remains *aporia*. Yet the nature of political power means that there will always be two distinct pedagogies: the assimilation to the nonviolent Jesus, servant of God and of "the least" in our midst, and a pedagogy of violence and worldly prudence in the state of which citizens are members. Christianity will remain a religious movement engaged in creative ethical and cultural work in each culture in which it finds itself only as it embraces both pedagogies simultaneously. But it starts and ends with the one pedagogy that defines its existence: discipleship. It will live and enact the best of its host society's culture and sense of citizenship, "in the Lord." In no other way can we educate future generations to work for the betterment (Christians would say "sanctity and righteousness") of the world.

8. Educating for Citizenship-Discipleship: Vamos Caminando: A Peruvian Catechism

Is it possible to teach ordinary Christians this sophisticated sense of discipleship-citizenship? I am convinced that it is just that toward which Paul's catechesis aims in the Pauline letters. Closer to our own time we have the splendid catechetical work of the pastoral team of Bambamarca (a city in the northern Andes of Peru), *Vamos Caminando*, to convince us that it is possible to combine the two pedagogies of discipleship and citizenship without losing or submerging the distinctive Christian voice.

I am not an expert in religious catechesis. Nor am I a specialist in the culture of the Peruvian Andes, although I have spent an extended time in the *altiplanos* of Bolivia and Peru. Yet I was stirred and moved to make applications to my own society and life as I read *Vamos Caminando's* social analysis, pictures, probing questions, scriptural narrative, Peruvian anecdote, and poetry.[66]

No one can mistake the implications for an active, critical self-determining citizenship based on a cooperative sense in themes: We are *Campesinos*. We work the land—but who benefits? Our community. Lima and the other cities exploit us—what can we do? Wanted: persons of determination. And you—have you made your decision yet? *Vamos Caminando* is replete with everyday stories about taking the bus to Lima, going to market, a bribe for the justice of the peace, community health, a wake service, fiestas, market prices, attempts to found cooperatives and do community organizing. These stories of civic work are woven into a concatenation of major Peruvian literary voices such as José Carlos Mariátegui and the novelist José María Arguedas as samples of the highest Peruvian ideals of citizenship and community. Nor does anyone miss the extent, in the stories and questions, and in the pictures and anecdotes, to which Peruvian society runs on the motor of dominative power and violence or the hints of how, at times, this power achieves some modicum of rational justice. The realities, dilemmas, and highest hopes of citizenship come fully to the fore in the text, rooted deeply in Peruvian culture.

This is the catechism for and from liberation theology. But does it reduce Christianity to a social movement? In a sense, much of the Old and the New Testament is read in the process of studying each of fifteen major units. In each chapter, a situation from real life, a dramatic Peruvian story, is constantly counterpoised with selections from the psalms, the prophets or the wisdom literature of the Old Testament, a Gospel narrative, or the letters of Paul. Each chapter moves the reader to a section entitled "Talking Points," which drives the respondent to move back and forth between the world of the New Testament and the everyday exercise of life and citizenship in the Peruvian *altiplano*. In addition to scripture texts, citations from church hymns, episcopal and papal social teaching all help the respondent to situate discipleship-citizenship in its rich ecclesial context of word and sacraments, community and service, worship, deep prayer, and thanksgiving.

In some units, the movement of the lesson plan goes from scriptural narrative to real-life situation, although most often, following the Latin American experience of Bible study and its application to real life in base communities, the directionality of the movement begins with real-life situations that evoke such feelings as puzzlement, anger, gratitude, wonder, joy, and outrage at injustice. This, after all, was the way Jesus taught. From real-life situations, not in a sacral language, Jesus moved to the heart of his Jewish tradition. As Carlos Mesters has argued, this pedagogical directionality is more likely to bring about the desired correlation between the ideals of discipleship and lived experience in citizenship than an alternative route of beginning in the scripture text itself, although Mesters does not absolutize the point.[67] Necessary for the success of this move from real-life anecdote and situation to the illumination of life by scripture is a rich sense and availability of the varied strands, themes, and texts of scripture which *Vamos Caminando* abundantly provides. Catechisms for discipleship-citizenship, as with the liturgical year of worship, must see to it that the wide cycle of the whole of the scriptures is followed.

Like any good pedagogy, *Vamos Caminando* expects its readers to take time to ponder and puzzle over pictures (accompanying each subunit), to appropriate the scriptures and their application to real life and to the real-life cases which test the mettle of discipleship. Finally, the key to pedagogy is application to our lives. Hence the importance of the anecdotes from real life which lie close to our own experiences. Finally, the full pedagogy moves toward dialogue within a believing community. It evokes an old and tested way of Christian pedagogy for a discipleship that shapes real life: *see* the real-life situation, *judge* it in the light of and according to the criterion of the scriptures, *act* accordingly in a praxis of discipleship. This pedagogy of Cardinal Cardijn's movement of Catholic workers and students in the period before and after World War II in Europe has been appropriated by Peruvian liberation theologians such as Gustavo Gutiérrez who began their ministry as chaplains in the Cardijn movement.[68]

There is little doubt in my mind about either the orthodoxy or the governing ideal of discipleship which controls the approach to social issues (utopian imagination, countercultural criticism, and constructive vocation) in *Vamos Caminando*. The guiding notes of the discipleship themes are clear in the chapter titles: "He died for us"; " 'Without love I am nothing' "; " 'Don't stand staring up at heaven!' "; "Awake!"; "Without love I am nothing."

Because it succeeds so brilliantly in bringing the New Testament to bear on ordinary Peruvian social realties, *Vamos Caminando* (like the New Testament itself) is, I presume, considered a dangerous document in Peru, evoking the opposition of both state authorities and elements in the church. As we have seen, discipleship is a way, an orthopraxis. It is also a doxology, an orthodoxy, a giving of praise and a worshiping of the true God whose delight is in humankind come fully alive (Irenaeus) and who rejoices in seeing widows, orphans, strangers, and *campesinos* in the land being brought into full citizenship rights as members of the community. I suspect that if we ever succeeded as religious educators in joining the two pedagogies of discipleship and citizenship in our own nation as well as does *Vamos Caminando*, we too would be forging a liberation theology for North America. Our pedagogy as religious educators would probably be seen as dangerous.

Ultimately, if we ever really put together the dangerous memory of Jesus and the dangerous memory of "the oecumene of suffering" which comprises the bulk of human history, even today, our form of citizenship would be creatively new, an ethical synthesis that would transform our society and its ordinary expectations. It would be one of the moments of *kairos* when the two pedagogies, like the lion and the lamb of the prophet, came together in peace. We deceive ourselves if we think we have any less dangerous goal in mind when we converse together as Christian educators about what we can do to educate the next generation of Christians to work for the betterment of the world.

NOTES

1. I am fully aware that hidden behind the two seemingly innocent concepts of citizenship and discipleship lies a whole series of controverted sociological and theological disputes about the correspondence between salvation or grace and history, the relation of church and state, and the locus of ethics and the discernment of God's purposes for history in the church and/or in the greater "secular" orders of creation.

2. Paul Ricoeur, *Politiek en Geloof: Essays van Paul Ricoeur*, ed. Ad. Peperzak (Utrecht: Ambo, 1968), p. 71.

3. D.W. Brogan, *Citizenship Today* (New York: Macmillan Co., 1963), p. 123.

4. H. Richard Niebuhr, *Christ and Culture* (New York: Harper & Brothers, 1951).

5. Robin W. Lovin, *Christian Faith and Public Choices: The Social Ethics of Barth, Brunner, and Bonhoeffer* (Philadelphia: Fortress Press, 1984), p. 3.

6. Robert N. Bellah et al., *Habits of the Heart: Individualism and Commitment in American Life* (Berkeley and Los Angeles: University of California Press, 1985).

7. Michael Walzer, *The Spheres of Justice: A Defense of Pluralism and Equality* (New York: Basic Books, 1983), p. 278. The essay "The Concept of Citizenship," on which I draw in this essay, is contained in Michael Walzer, *Obligations: Essays on Disobedience, Wars, and Citizenship* (New York: Basic Books, 1977).

8. Bertrand de Jouvenel, *On Power: Its Nature and the History of Its Growth* (Boston: Beacon Press, 1968), p. 37.

9. Ricoeur, *Politiek*, pp. 32–51.

10. Ibid., p. 32.

11. In this regard, it may be important to note that most sociological pleas for a vigorous civil religion as a cement for public consensus rest on utilitarian social arguments. Religion is celebrated and used for the purposes of—an admittedly often truncated—citizenship with scant regard to its deeper purposes and meanings which transcend citizenship.

12. Walzer, *Spheres*, p. 246.

13. Ibid., p. 304.

14. Ibid., p. 247.

15. See Richard John Neuhaus, *The Naked Public Square: Religion and Democracy in America* (Grand Rapids, Mich.: Wm. B. Eerdmans Publishing Co., 1984).

16. The two Tocqueville citations are from his correspondence with Madame Swetchine and Arthur de Gobineau in *Opera Omnia*, vol. 5, as

cited in John A. Coleman, "The Christian as Citizen," *Commonweal* 110, no. 15 (9 September 1983): 457–62.

17. Walzer, *Spheres*, p. 308.

18. Ricoeur, *Politiek*, p. 82.

19. Jon Sobrino, *Christology at the Crossroads: A Latin American Approach* (Maryknoll, N.Y.: Orbis Books, 1978), p. xxii.

20. Ibid., p. xxiii.

21. Ibid., p. 91.

22. Jürgen Moltmann, *The Crucified God* (New York: Harper & Row, 1974).

23. John Howard Yoder, *The Politics of Jesus* (Grand Rapids, Mich.: Wm. B. Eerdmans Publishing Co., 1972).

24. Theological differences about the extent to which structures of sin have been surmounted in Jesus' resurrection, and the power of grace actually to transform persons and structures, lie behind the different positions of Sobrino and Yoder. Yoder's "Christ against culture" model assumes little real transformation in and through the resurrection and lays a stronger accent on the not-yet quality of the breakthrough of the kingdom than is true of Sobrino's "Christ transforming" model.

25. Edward Schillebeeckx, *Gerechtigheid en Liefde: Genade en Beurijding* (Bloemendael, The Netherlands: H. Nelissen, 1977), pp. 514–20. Cf. the Pauline doctrine of a struggle with the power in Ephesians 6:11–12 and Revelation 13, where, manifestly, the "powers" find incarnation in states and regimes.

26. Reinhold Niebuhr, *The Nature and Destiny of Man*, 2 vols. (New York: Charles Scribner's Sons, 1947 and 1955).

27. Walzer, *Spheres*, p. 310.

28. Ibid., p. 63.

29. Ibid., p. 6.

30. Ibid., p. 9.

31. Ibid., p. 314.

32. Ibid., p. 281.

33. Ibid., p. 314.

34. Ibid., p. 318.

35. Bellah et al., *Habits of the Heart*, p. 200.

36. Cf. ibid., pp. 200–203.

37. Ibid., p. 217.

38. Ibid., p. 218.

39. Ibid., p. 295.

40. Ibid., p. 335.

41. Ricoeur, *Politiek*, p. 82.

42. Ibid., p. 87.
43. Schillebeeckx, *Gerechtigheid*, p. 65.
44. Ricoeur, *Politiek*, p. 35.
45. Schillebeeckx, *Gerechtigheid*, p. 715.
46. Walzer, *Spheres*, p. 45.
47. Chap. 1, "Medemens en Naaste," in Ricoeur, *Politiek*.
48. Ricoeur, *Politiek*, p. 158.
49. "Justice in the World," par. 6, in *Renewing the Earth: Catholic Documents on Peace, Justice and Liberation*, ed. David J. O'Brien and Thomas A. Shannon (Garden City, N.Y.: Doubleday & Co., Image Books, 1977).
50. "Justice in the World," par 35.
51. Paul VI, in *Documentation Catholique* 74 (1977): 307.
52. For a broader discussion of the issues in these paragraphs, see Dermot A. Lane, *Foundations for Social Theology: Praxis, Process and Salvation* (New York: Paulist Press, 1984).
53. On Christian political parties, see Schillebeeckx, *Gerechtigheid*, pp. 718–28.
54. Ricoeur, *Politiek*, p. 86.
55. Cf. Schillebeeckx, *Gerechtigheid*, pp. 34–56.
56. Lovin, *Christian Faith*, p. 139.
57. Louis van Bladel, S.J., *Christelijk Geloof en MaatschappijKritiek* (Antwerp: De Nederlandsche Boekhandel, 1985).
58. Ricoeur, *Politiek*, p. 198 (my trans.).
59. Cf. van Bladel, *Christelijk Geloof,* chap. 6, "Maatschappelijk-Ethische Beleving van het Christelijk Geloof."
60. Ricoeur, *Politiek*, p. 103.
61. Ibid., pp. 29–30.
62. Ibid.
63. Schillebeeckx, *Gerechtigheid*, p. 534.
64. Cf. ibid., pp. 524–27.
65. Ibid., p. 539.
66. Pastoral team of Bambamarca, *Vamos Caminando: A Peruvian Catechism*, trans. John Metcalf (London: SCM Press, 1985).
67. Carlos Mesters, "The Use of the Bible in Christian Communities of the Common People," in *The Challenge of Basic Christian Communities*, ed. Sergio Torres and John Eagleson (Maryknoll, N.Y.: Orbis Books, 1981), pp. 197–213.
68. I am indebted for the information about Gutiérrez's connection with the Cardijn movement to an interview held in Bolivia with a colleague of his in the 1960s in Peru, Sister Barbara Hendrix, M.M.

PART II

Fundamental Theological and Educational Views

3

Basic Christian Understandings

Bernard J. Cooke

U NDERGIRDING THE DISCUSSION in this volume of discipleship and citizenship lies an educational question: What do Christians need to know in order to become disciples? In his essay, Don Browning argues for the centrality of practical moral thinking grounded in an ethics of principle and of character. I would like to take an even more inclusive view, proposing a theological framework structured on five fundamentals: (1) the church, (2) Jesus the Christ, (3) the God who saves, (4) divine/human communication, and (5) authentic Christian life.

Research during the past few decades has indicated the extent to which various contexts of religious education are governed by different purposes and therefore demand varying pedagogical approaches, even at times varying content matter.[1] What is needed for a catechism class of ten-year-olds is obviously not what is required for an adult education group. But what is common to all situations of religious instruction is the goal of *understanding* what religion, specifically Christianity, is all about.[2]

Having said this, one must immediately introduce a clarification: the term "understanding" can be used quite ambiguously. One can use the word to refer to a purely informational bit of knowledge: one knows that a certain denomination explains an element of belief, for example, the human need for grace, in a particular way. Anyone, with or without religious faith, can possess this kind of understanding. Or one can, with faith in the teaching role of his or her church, accept that church's doctrinal formulations about divine grace as true. Or one can understand with some accuracy the reality to which the formulation points, that is, the gracious intervention of God in human affairs. The last instance requires, of course, a certain element of personal religious experience, grounded in faith but occurring as part of one's awareness of life.

While all three instances of understanding have their place, it is the third instance, personal understanding of the reality of God acting in human life, that is the ideal which religious education tries to achieve.[3] In such understanding, one does not simply know about God as revealed in Jesus the Christ; one knows this God.

Without retreating from the position that this personal understanding of the realities accepted in faith should be the objective of religious education, we must recognize the danger involved in this stance. The danger is that people will drift toward an uncritical, imprecise religious feeling about God; that they will be content with quite inaccurate understandings of their faith. Theoretical study of education, specifically of religious education, has in recent years stressed the interaction of cognition, affectivity, and action and the necessary contribution of each to balanced personal development. The influence of Jean Piaget and Paulo Freire has been basic but by no means isolated.[4]

The desired goal, then, combines the two elements, experience of reality and accurate knowledge. One could refer to this as "an educated understanding" of one's faith but with the proviso that one is not necessarily referring to any sophisticated technical explanation. More than one sophisticated explanation is faulty, and many a simple and direct grasp of religious beliefs is accurate. Such accurate explanations, however, exist only because of some competent religious instruction that was guided, at least indirectly, by careful theological scholarship.

The purpose of the present essay is to deal with this kind of religious understanding, to discuss five elements of down-to-earth knowledge that people need in order to deal religiously with the experienced reality of their human life. This need has long been recognized by church groups and responded to by their production of educational materials to help achieve this goal. Actually the history of such efforts goes back at least as far as Luther's catechism. My essay will limit itself to Christian congregational education, though one could speak similarly about other situations of Christian instruction or about instruction in other religions. My basic presupposition is that people need relatively few basic religious understandings; but these few must be true.

1. The Church

An essay such as the present one almost inevitably deals with Christian understandings in propositional form. It describes the content of belief in formulated statements that rather starkly lay out the claims that Christianity has made about God, about Jesus as the Christ, and about itself as a path of human salvation. Yet we know that people's actual awareness of their Christian faith and life is not cast in such abstract and certain forms: people's understanding of Christianity and their consequent self-identification as Christian is often a mixture of piecemeal information, folk tradition, civil religion, and authentic openness to the gospel mixed with questions and ever. doubts. Formal religious education has in many cases made a substantial contribution, but the experience of being part of a Christian congregation has informally imparted the awareness of Christianity that is basically operative in most people's faith. "There is simply nothing as successful or as powerful in communicating messages as a community itself. One learns religious messages through models and through memories."[5]

If this is so, the importance of accurate understanding about the church is evident; and this means personal understanding of the actual congregational situation of which they are a part. While some knowledge of the nature and operation of "the great church" is needed, for most people it is their local Christian community that is church for them. This is where people find themselves with other Christians who are more or less like-minded; it is a center of organizing works of ministry; it is the context for most, if not all, of their public worship; it is that with which they immediately identify when they think of themselves as "religious." At times they will be involved in activity at the synod or diocese or presbytery level, or be affected by decisions taken at that level. However, most of their experience of being Christian occurs in their congregation; and indications are that the role of the local situation will increase rather than diminish in the years ahead.

As is the case with almost everything else, Christians' view of the church has undergone considerable change in the years since World War II. Perhaps the most publicized shift occurred in Roman Catholicism when Vatican II insisted that the church is the entire people; but much the same awakening to the importance of the laity had begun earlier in Protestant circles.[6] This represents much more than a shift in theological emphasis and theoretical understanding; it is a basic change in Christian self-identity, a broadening of both responsibility and power. However, the responsibility will be faced and the power exercised in truly Christian fashion only if women and men understand accurately the mission of the church in history and the kind of power that is appropriate to the pursuit of that mission.

To those whose religious practice is relatively minimal and perfunctory this provokes no questions; they are content with their once-a-week (or less frequent) contact with Christianity. But for those seriously interested in Christian discipleship it has led to problems. At times they find the institutional structures of the church a burden, even an obstacle to what they feel the church should be and do. It is such people who need to understand why the structured church is necessary, why "institutionless Christianity" is an illusory ideal; who need to grasp the deeper reality of the church as the body of Christ; and who in a new way need to identify "the church" as themselves.

Devoted Christians must be helped to live with the human inadequacies of church structures; but something more fundamental is at stake. The experience of being Christian should be the experience of being a disciple of Christ and, along with one's fellow Christians, the body of Christ. Clearly, people cannot have such an experience if they do not understand what these terms mean. They need not be given a complicated technical explanation—Paul used the notions in dealing with communities of relatively uneducated people. However, people do need to have some grasp of the mystery dimension of Christianity and some grasp of the way in which they as disciples of Christ form part of that mystery.

Too often "the church" has been explained to Christians as equivalent with the official levels of the church and as an indispensable intermediary between them and God—even though the general thrust of the sixteenth-century Reformation (and of much that preceded it) was in the opposite direction. Too many Christians have not known the vivid, life-changing, and often painful experience of consciously participating in a community of believers who, as Walter Brueggemann describes, articulate an alternative view of the world and of the living God.[7] What needs to be taught is that the church is not that through which Christians pass in order to reach God, but that it is they themselves who are the context of the divine presence. The church is the situation in which they are meant to encounter God. The reign of God is in their midst.

2. *Jesus the Christ*

Such an approach to understanding the Christian church should make it clear that correct understanding about Jesus of Nazareth is basic to Christian faith. The only ultimately distinguishing element of Christianity as a religion is the identity and role of Jesus. If he is not what Christians claim him to be, Christianity has little right to exist. Yet a random questioning of those who consider themselves Christian would reveal amazingly diverse and vague opinions about this Jesus. All would possess some knowledge that there was a historical person who lived roughly two thousand years ago, who taught, performed works of healing, and was unjustly put to death by the combined leadership of the Jews and the Romans. Some would add that Jesus is "the son of God" but would then be unable to give any precise content to this title. Most would become even less certain of their understandings if asked about the reality of Jesus' resurrection—which, incidentally, is the central element in the original Christian kerygma. And if one

asked whether Jesus still exists humanly and, if so, how and
where, one would probably encounter puzzled silence.

One begins to wonder what is meant by Christianity being a
faith community, that is, a sharing of belief in Jesus as Christ and
Lord, when one observes this lack of common understanding as
to who and what Jesus really was and is. Are people in an
ordinary congregation truly sharing a common view about
Jesus' identity and role in human life?

What is disturbing is not that such a cacophony of voices exists
but that so little attention has been paid to it. Though biblical
and theological research have for some decades been focused on
Christology,[8] there is still little awareness on the congregational
or catechetical level that people need to discover the real Jesus,
that their present understandings need correction or at the very
least augmenting. Much more than theoretical knowledge about
doctrine is involved; Christian prayer and Christian discipleship
should be directed to the reality of the risen Christ, not to some
"imagined Jesus."

Though we have only limited ability to reach back two thousand years and recover the historical circumstances into which
Jesus of Nazareth was born and with which he interacted, we do
have some possibilities of appreciating how Jesus' contempo-
raries saw him. Despite the fact that the New Testament literature views Jesus, including his historical career, in the light of
the Easter experience, we can gain some insight into what Jesus
was actually like and into what he actually taught and did.[9]

Circumscribed though our accurate knowledge of the historical figure Jesus is, it contains elements that are of immense
importance to Christians' down-to-earth religious beliefs. The
extraordinary ordinariness of Jesus, his refusal to exercise institutionalized political power, his friendship with and concern
for the marginated of society, his fidelity to the prophetic vocation that was his, his view of God as irrevocably compassionate,
the unassuming dignity that was his because of his radical honesty, the passionate commitment to bettering the lives of people,
that is, establishing God's new community—these are aspects of
Jesus that are fundamental to one's understanding of what it
seems to be Christian. Without our knowing this, there is no

possibility of following Paul's admonition to "put on the mind of Christ Jesus."[10]

Christianity's understanding of Jesus is not confined, however, to knowledge about his roughly thirty-five years of earthly life. The Jesus about whom the New Testament speaks, the Jesus to whom Christian faith from its very beginnings has been directed, is the risen Christ, the Lord of glory.[11] And if there are difficulties in acquiring accurate knowledge about the historical Jesus, these difficulties are magnified when a faith community attempts to grasp the reality of the risen Jesus, the Christ. But at the very least, Christians' knowledge about and faith awareness of Jesus as the Christ in our lives should be guided by those elements of earliest Christianity's faith experience which underlie the New Testament literature.

Admittedly there are problems in interpreting those Gospel passages we refer to as "the apparitions of the risen Christ," but beneath the literary forms in which the primitive Christian faith is couched there lie certain basic beliefs that are normative for subsequent generations of believers: Jesus is *alive;* Jesus is *humanly* alive, though in some different situation of human existing; Jesus remains *in relationship* with those who accept Christ in faith—as a matter of fact, there is a life bond that unites Christians with Jesus; in his new *fulfilled* situation Jesus enters into the definitive stage of his ministry, because he can now share with others the full power of his Spirit which is his God's Spirit also.

Granted that these elements of belief do not provide a detailed insight into what "resurrection" is for Jesus, and thereafter for others also, they at least give some authentically traditional guidelines for Christians who wish to form a deepening relationship with Christ. Having to discipline their religious imagination so that it does not exceed the evidence about the risen Christ provided by mainstream Christian tradition will help condition people to resist the ultimate religious temptation, which is to think about God according to their own images and likenesses.

Unless there is careful reflection about the divine, there is no hope that Christians will be able to deal accurately with the two-thousand-year-old Christian claims about the divinity of Jesus.

What does it mean to say that Jesus is God's own Son, that Jesus shares full divinity with God the Father, that Jesus is—according to the great conciliar creeds from Nicaea to Chalcedon—"consubstantial in divinity" with the transcendent God? How can Christians believe that Jesus is "a divine person," one of the Trinity, and still be monotheists?

Obviously, nothing is gained by trying to tell people in the pews about "divine processions" or "spiration," about the refinements of dogmatic language that led finally to terms like "hypostatic union," about medieval and modern theology's complicated attempts to discover grounds for asserting non-contradiction in Christian teaching about divine trinity. Perhaps it would be better to lead people to some realization that there is a depth in the personhood of Jesus that somehow opens onto the divine, and that at this point our ordinary human understandings break down. Perhaps the only positive understanding we possess and can communicate is that Jesus stands in unique personal relationship to the God whose transcendence we cannot grasp but can only point to. At the very least, we should not leave people with the misconception that they understand more than they do when they refer to Jesus as "the Son of God."

3. The God Who Saves

One who accepts the teaching of Jesus is led inescapably to the ineffable mystery of the infinite God, for it is about this God whom Jesus experienced as "Abba" that Jesus constantly spoke. But what should Christians be told about God? A simple and very important response would be: tell them what Jesus taught about God. However, in today's world simple repetition of Jesus' teaching is not sufficient. We need to plumb that teaching to discover the implied response to the questions that modern critical thought has raised with regard to the human being's ability to deal with the existence and nature of the divine.

For a relatively small group of people it is important to reflect philosophically about our human ability to know the divine in itself. For the bulk of people in the average congregation it is more practical to assume the existence of God, to bypass sophisticated questions about the reality of God-in-self, and to concentrate on what biblical faith and Christian tradition hand on as "revelation," that is, God-for-us.

What this requires is explaining the Christian understanding of salvation. What is it that God is doing in human lives to enable men and women to reach their destiny? In our world with its absorption of the scientific mentality into even our common-sense view of the realities that surround us, the rather naive understandings of "divine providence" that prevailed in former times are no longer acceptable. Indeed, the question "What is meant by divine providence?" may be the most radical religious question facing us today. In the wake of scientific advances, the very notion of salvation is questioned; many people see secular solutions as adequate to individual and societal needs. At the same time, there is widening disillusionment with the "solutions" offered by contemporary science and technology and an obvious retreat by many to a religious and cultural fundamentalism. Again, there is a widespread challenge to Christianity's teaching about salvation that comes—at least in the affluent "first world"—from consumerism, the absorbing quest for possessing things, the promise that having the latest style and gimmick will bring happiness, the demand for instant satisfaction of "needs" that for the most part are artificially created by advertising.

Actually, an effective explanation of salvation must deal with two issues: the nature of the evil from which human beings need to be saved and the manner in which God helps human beings overcome this evil. Science's challenge has forced us to confront both these matters in a new way, but a way that promises to be truly religious. Because of modern psychological insights we have greater clarity about the forces that work to diminish our human personhood. Because of sociological research we understand better the institutional forms and procedures by which human beings are opposed and harmed. Drawing from such knowledge, Christian faith can now go a step farther in understanding both individual and social sin.[12]

For a number of reasons, it is of great practical importance that people develop a more accurate understanding of sin. It is not enough to criticize the excessively negative approach to human moral behavior that for so many centuries characterized Christian discussion about sin. An alternative and more balanced

insight into human culpability is needed so that today's Christians can face life's responsibilities with maturity and without
anxiety.[13]

On the individual level, it is important to recover some of the
biblical perspective of sin as infidelity and folly and refusal to
accept the dependence that is intrinsic to creaturehood. On the
public level, Christians today need to regain the prophetic insight into the evil of social oppression and injustice, not only
admitting that such things are evil but discovering the manner in
which such evils are systematized in the institutions and embed-
ded in the prejudices of modern societies.[14] Drawing on Walter
Brueggemann's language, "bilingual" Christians whose reading
of reality is shaped "behind the wall" through recollection of
their particular experiences of pain and hope can then engage in
the public language "on the wall" with heightened sensitivity to
structural oppression.[15]

While the universal human experiences of suffering and death
must be dealt with, and human effort must continue to be
directed toward reducing suffering as far as possible, a Christian
perspective cannot see either suffering or death as ultimate evil.
Even for those engaged in the healing professions, death should
not be viewed as defeat and its avoidance the primary objective.
Evil strikes at human beings most basically when it diminishes
or even destroys the personal dimension of people's lives.[16]

What Christians need is not some theoretical attempt to reconcile the existence of evil with the existence of a good God.
Rather, they need to appreciate what the real evils are that
threaten their humanity in today's world, what the "real sins"
are that stand as barriers to people reaching their destiny; and
they need to understand what concretely constitutes salvation
from these evils. What, for example, can be done to save the
starving peoples of the earth from the tragic human indignity
that goes along with abject impoverishment, and what can be
done to save affluent peoples from the spiritual dullness that
prevents them from being bothered by the fact that their high
level of economic well-being is bought at the expense of others'
starvation?

In this arena of good struggling with evil, what is God's role in
saving humanity? What, on the other hand, are human beings

expected to do as their share in saving themselves? Obviously we are here confronted with the age-old question of faith and good works but in terms of the concrete circumstances and responsibilities of people who call themselves Christian. People need to understand what it is that God is doing in their lives if they are to cooperate with this divine action.

It is always perilous to suggest that we today have a more correct and workable understanding of Christian life than our predecessors in the faith. But it does seem that a somewhat new and more understandable approach to "grace" has come to the fore in recent theology: an approach that sees God's self-revealing presence in the consciousness of believers as a radically transforming force that is capable of saving them and through their actions saving others as well. This perspective is, of course, very biblical;[17] the New Testament writings are filled with it—for example, the application of "Emmanuel" ("God with us") to Jesus in the infancy narrative, Luke's theology of Jesus as replacement of the temple, and the prologue of John and its notion of the divine Word dwelling with us. However, this biblical view needs to be translated into people's understanding of how God dwells with them in *today's world*, of how God's presence is meant to transform individuals and society, and of what is expected of human beings in response to God's presence.

4. Divine/Human Communication

A more adequate understanding of grace leads us logically to the fourth area of understanding that is needed as ground for Christians' living out their faith. When one speaks of "presence," one is referring to a reality that comes into being when one person communicates with another, when somehow the "speaker" inhabits the consciousness of the "hearer." In the case of Christians dealing with the God revealed in Jesus, the open hearing of the word of God is faith. But in saying this, one must remain aware that the Word is incarnated in the risen Christ and that "hearing the word" is a matter of establishing personal friendship with Christ.[18]

For Christians to develop this kind of relationship with Christ and through Christ with God, they must have an understanding of *prayer.* What kind of communication can actually take place between God and human beings, and what is the risen Jesus' role in such interchange?

One thing that does have to be highlighted in explaining the nature of prayer to people is that the initiative in divine/human communication is always on the divine side. Contrary to people's ordinary view, God does not answer our prayers—at least in the way we think God does. We tend to think we turn to God in prayer and God then responds. Such a position of response would, of course, imply that we effect a change in God, something that philosophical reflection about the transcendent tells us is incompatible with divine reality. Beyond philosophy, biblical revelation insists that God takes the initiative: it is God who unexpectedly calls Moses, who does the same with the great charismatic prophets, who is described as going out to search for sinful Israel and bring about reconciliation of the people and God. The New Testament is no less explicit: God so loved the world that God sent God's own Son (John 3:16); the good shepherd goes out to seek the lost sheep (John 10); and the book of Revelation describes God standing at the door and knocking.

Very simply, God speaks first and Christian prayer is a response to that divine word. That implies, however, that people must realize how and where and when God speaks. The Bible occupies, of course, a privileged place as word of God; but the history of biblical interpretation proves that understanding what God is saying through these texts is far from obvious. While the average man or woman of faith need not be acquainted with the latest advances of scriptural research, their personal use of the Bible should be guided by responsible modern scholarship.[19] If we are to hear the Bible as God's word, it is critically important to extract meaning from the texts rather than reading our own presuppositions into them.

Beyond the scriptural word, however, there are other situations that faith sees as communication from God to humanity. Liturgical worship should function in this way; actually, it should provide the paradigmatic occasion for proclaiming, hearing, and responding to the biblical word. Both Protestantism and Catholicism are today recovering their traditions about the evangelical dimension of liturgy, something that should lead to increased experience and appreciation of liturgy as communal prayer that is also deeply personal.

Paradoxically, at a time when spiritual values are disappearing from many contexts of human life there seems to be a widening interest in prayer. However one wishes to evaluate them, the huge audiences listening to electronic preachers, the worldwide spread of the charismatic movement, the attraction to the person and thought of Thomas Merton, the fascination of so many for Eastern contemplation—all are symptoms of a desire and search for genuine personal contact with the divine. But if Christians are to pray authentically, to come into real relation with the true God, they need to be guided by those who themselves understand what it means to pray as a Christian.

Most basically, people need to understand how the happenings of their lives are truly "word of God." This does not mean that they should come to see these daily experiences as a series of "little miracles" that God is specially working for them—such a view may be pious, but it is erroneous. Rather, they need to be led to the understanding that all created existence is grounded in the divine self-giving, that human life is permeated by God's invitation to accept divine presence, and that the Spirit of God does indeed work wherever human beings are deeply concerned for one another's well-being.[20] If awareness of this pervading presence of God is nurtured, it will lead naturally to prayerful response. Indeed, the awareness is itself the most basic response.

5. Authentic Christian Life

A fifth area of understanding is even more down-to-earth: What does one mean by the term "a good Christian"? There have been times when this term was applied to any morally respectable person, independent really of any genuinely religious faith. More recently, particularly with renewed interest in and knowledge of the New Testament writings, we recognize that "being Christian" is more than just "being ethically good," though it obviously includes the latter. But what precisely is one expected to do in order to be "a good Christian," a follower of "the way"?

Basic to any response to this question is an understanding of "sin," "guilt," and "conscience," three terms whose meaning has been seriously challenged these past few decades. Earlier in this essay we studied the way in which a more accurate insight into sin is required in order to grasp the meaning of "salvation." But a correct view of sin is needed also if Christian experience of guilt is to be honest and balanced. While there is no doubt that some past generations focused excessively on human sinfulness, to the point of creating neurotic guilt feelings in many Christians, the existence of sin is a reality of human life that must be acknowledged and maturely handled. In a "Christianity come of age" the idea of sin needs to be demythologized; but that does not say that its reality should be denied. While the full notion of sin can be appreciated only in a context of faith, the fact of human sinful activity is only too clearly evidenced in human experience.

Biblical studies have recently contributed a great deal to clarifying our understanding of sin. Sin as *alienation*, already a basic category in Old Testament thought, is not too difficult to grasp without referring directly to God. But sin as *infidelity*, though necessarily understood by reference to human relationships in which betrayal occurs, can find its full meaning only in terms of the gratuitous love of God being stupidly refused by human beings. To the person who has pondered the prophetic designation of Israel's sinfulness as "adultery," any description of sin as simply violation of laws, even God's laws, is most inadequate. More is involved than obtaining an accurate view of sin; seeing sin as infidelity to human and divine love makes it possible to move toward realistic and effective conversion for conversion consists basically in choosing to love oneself, others, and God. This does not imply that conversion is easy, but at least one knows what one has to do, which is the indispensable first step toward doing it.

Today, thanks in large part to advances in psychology, we understand better the complex dynamics that underlie people's moral behavior. We are less prone to attribute ethically deviant actions to malice or bad will, because we are conscious that social conditioning or psychological imbalance can limit some people's culpability. This is all to the good; it helps keep us from rash judgment of others and contributes to a more realistic appraisal of our own behavior. But at the same time, we need to avoid the extreme of attributing all misbehavior to psychological compulsion or environmental impact. Sin is a reality; perhaps it is not as pervasive as some earlier generations thought, but sin is still one of the key determinants in human affairs. And when persons sin, the appropriate Christian awareness—as a matter of fact, the sane response—is a sense of guilt.

Here, again, there is an area of important personal understanding with which religious education must deal. Christians must know clearly that true guilt is a conscious judgment that one has done something seriously wrong, that one has harmed oneself or other human beings, and that in so doing one has been unfaithful to the love relationship with God in Christ to which one is pledged by Christian baptism. Authentic guilt is not an anxiety-ridden guilt feeling; it is an honest and mature judgment that one has done wrong, an admission of moral failure, grounded in the resolve to do otherwise in the future.

Perhaps the best pedagogical approach to explaining the reality of "guilt" is to concentrate on people's *responsibility*. The positive knowledges and attitudes that education tries to contribute to a person's moral development have to do with grasping the ways in which one can and should respond to the challenges of life. Unless people understand accurately the responsibilities they bear as Christians, they cannot become aware of the irresponsibility they incur in shirking or refusing these responsibilities.

But should not truly Christian behavior go beyond avoidance of sin, beyond the correct social behavior expected of any person? One clear way of responding to this question is in terms of *discipleship*. A Christian should in his or her life translate the example of Jesus into actions needed in our world. However, it would be a mistake to understand "disciple of Christ" as one who *succeeds* Jesus in the ministry he carried on two millennia ago. Rather, since Christians in community are truly the body of Christ, discipleship is a matter of co-working with the risen Christ who still is present in Spirit to the human history that Christ seeks to transform. To be a disciple of Christ, to be truly a Christian, a person must allow the direction of the Spirit to be the norm for his or her choices and actions; one must be faithful to Christ's Spirit.

No doubt about it—this approach to judging which behavior is appropriately Christian is less absolute, and for that reason less comfortable, than an approach in terms of obeying specified laws. It is not only less clear-cut; it is more demanding, for it involves the total personal response of a Christian and not just this or that particular element of behavior.

But because they are so open-ended and encompassing, the demands of discipleship need to be spelled out somewhat for people who must live in the actual circumstances of today's world. This is an element of religious education that must continue throughout the adult life of a Christian, an element that must be supplied within the context of a congregation; it will not be supplied elsewhere. Sunday sermons, adult education programs, special lecture series—all need to work together to indicate to people the practical dictates of Christian faith in our rapidly changing world.

John Coleman's essay in this volume offers recommendations toward a pedagogy for Christian "disciple-citizens." The two roles are distinct yet closely interrelated, and religious education must help nurture both aspects. Coleman categorizes the unique contributions of citizenship to discipleship as a wider solidarity, a humbler service, and a new reality test for responsibility, while discipleship contributes to citizenship the important perspectives of utopia, counterculture, and vocation.[21] Living this double role is certain to involve many complex and controversial choices; and as Coleman maintains, an effective pedagogy for discipleship-citizenship would be both creative and dangerous.[22]

At a time when Christian ministry has taken on a broader meaning, when in all the churches ministerial activity is shared with a widening group of the nonordained, there is increased need to develop people's ability to discern the Christian course of action in their professional, familial, and public life. Orthopraxis is now seen to parallel orthodoxy as a basic criterion for judging the genuineness of people's faith. This in no way detracts from the importance of correct understanding, which my essay has tried to emphasize. Any appraisal of what it means to act as "a good Christian" will be controlled by one's understanding of Jesus as the Christ, of the church, of God's saving grace, and of Christian discipleship. Understanding of itself will not suffice. Knowledge is not virtue, but authentic Christian faith and life exist correlative to an accurate understanding of the gospel.

NOTES

1. This is reflected, for example, in the theme symposia published in *Religious Education* which have dealt with special groups such as adults or adolescents. See vols. 74/3 (1979), 76/4 (1981), 80/1 (1985), and 81/2 (1986).

2. This is not to deny that understanding is sought for the purpose of more authentic religious behavior. "Orthopraxis" has become more prominent as a formal criterion of genuine Christian faith. But there is a commonsense recognition that people's actions are correlative to what they know. An interesting interchange on the role of cognition in religious education is provided by Charles Melchert, " 'Understanding' as a Purpose of Religious Education," *Religious Education* 76 (1981), pp. 178–86 and the response of Craig Dykstra, *Vision and Character: A Christian Educator's Alternative to Kohlberg* (New York: Paulist Press, 1981), pp. 187–94.

3. Such religious education is quite different from the "religious studies" that are pursued in college or university. The latter are on principle confined to description or analysis that brackets the truth claims of the religion being studied. For an indication of the extent to which the relation of such religious studies to theology or to religious education is still uncertain and debated, one could examine the presidential addresses given to the national convention of the American Academy of Religion in 1977 by Schubert Ogden ("Theology and Religious Studies: Their Difference and the Difference It Makes," *Journal of the American Academy of Religion* 46 [1978]: 3–18) and in 1979 by Langdon Gilkey ("The AAR and the Anxiety of Nonbeing: An Analysis of Our Present Cultural Situation," *Journal of the American Academy of Religion* 48 [1980]: 5–18).

4. For a thorough discussion of the issue and a critical absorption of the insights of Freire and Piaget, see Thomas H. Groome, *Christian Religious Education: Sharing Our Story and Vision* (New York: Harper & Row, 1980).

5. Irving Greenberg, "From Modernity to Post-Modernity: Community and the Revitalization of Traditional Religion," *Religious Education* 73 (1978): 449–69.

6. Cf. chap. 2 in the *Dogmatic Constitution on the Church* in Austin Flannery, ed., *Vatican Council II; The Conciliar and Post Conciliar Documents*, vol. 1, new rev. ed. (Collegeville, Minn.: Liturgical Press, 1984); and sec. 6 of *The Evanston Report: The Second Assembly of the World Council of Churches* (New York: Harper & Bros., 1955), on the 1954 meeting of the World Council of Churches.

7. See, in this volume, Walter Brueggemann, "The Legitimacy of a Sectarian Hermeneutic: 2 Kings 18—19," pp.13–26, on the alternative reality articulated by the legitimate sectarian community.

8. Cf. Bernard Cooke, "Horizons on Christology in the Seventies," *Horizons* 6 (1979): 193–217. Probably the most comprehensive synthesis of recent exegetical and theological research is the two-volume work of Edward Schillebeeckx: *Jesus: An Experiment in Christology* (New York: Crossroad, 1979), and *Christ: The Experience of Jesus as Lord* (New York: Crossroad, 1980). On Christology and religious education, see Reginald Fuller, "The Nature and Function of New Testament Christology," in *Emerging Issues in Religious Education*, ed. Gloria Durka and Joanmarie Smith (New York: Paulist Press, 1976).

9. While textual methodologies, form, source, and redaction criticism have made a major contribution, a rich new body of insight has come with more sociological studies, such as Gerd Theissen, *Sociology of Early Palestinian Christianity* (Philadelphia: Fortress Press, 1978), and John G. Gager, *Kingdom and Community: The Social World of Early Christianity* (Englewood Cliffs, N.J.: Prentice-Hall, 1975).

10. In his essay in this volume, "The Two Pedagogies: Discipleship and Citizenship," John Coleman summarizes the crucial aspects of Jesus' ministry for discipleship as (1) "decisive dispositions" such as surrender to the Father, self-sacrificing love, and option for the poor; (2) "crucial paradigmatic actions: such as foot washing, healing, the cross, and forgiveness; and (3) a utopian teaching related to the reign of God" in parables, narratives, and teaching sayings. Coleman cautions, however, that discipleship is not mere imitation of Jesus' actions but a "metanormative ethic" to be applied to one's own context (pp. 45–48). See my discussion of "authentic Christian life," pp. 91–95.

11. This is not to accept the excessive dichotomy, made by some New Testament scholars, between "the Jesus of history" and "the Christ of faith." Several recent studies, e.g., Michael Cook, *The Jesus of Faith: A Study in Christology* (New York: Paulist Press, 1981), have highlighted the experiential continuity of Jesus' disciples: the Jesus experienced in their Easter consciousness was the Jesus they had known during his public ministry.

12. Both the broad and diversified development of psychology of religion and the emergence of "political theology" (including "theology of liberation") constitute major resources for religious education in this regard. For a cross-sectional view of the recent impact of study in the

psychology of religion, see Peter Homans, ed., *The Dialogue Between Theology and Psychology* (Chicago: University of Chicago Press, 1968). An introduction to "theology of liberation" is provided by Robert McAfee Brown, *Theology in a New Key: Responding to Liberation Themes* (Philadelphia: Westminster Press, 1978).

13. On the development of mature moral responsibility, see Walter Conn, *Conscience* (Birmingham, Ala.: Religious Education Press, 1981).

14. See, e.g., Peter L. Berger, *Pyramids of Sacrifice: Political Ethics and Social Change* (New York: Basic Books, 1974). While they do not deal directly with ethical judgment, Richard J. Barnet and Ronald E. Müller, *Global Reach: The Power of the Multinational Corporations* (New York: Simon & Schuster, 1974), present a compelling picture of the massive institutional forces that operate to oppress millions in today's world.

15. See, in this volume, Brueggemann, "The Legitimacy of a Sectarian Hermeneutic," esp. pp. 26–29.

16. Interestingly, Edward Schillebeeckx in *Christ* focuses both the initial Christian "Easter experience" and present-day application of that experience on the phenomenon of human suffering and on the salvation from suffering which Christianity is meant to implement.

17. Cf. Samuel Terrien, *The Elusive Presence: Toward a New Biblical Theology* (San Francisco: Harper & Row, 1978).

18. Probably no contemporary thinker has provided more profound insight into the notion of hearing the word of God than has Karl Rahner, particularly in his *Hearers of the Word* (New York: Herder & Herder, 1969).

19. Cf. Mary C. Boys, "Religious Education and Contemporary Biblical Scholarship," *Religious Education* 74 (1979): 182–97. She points out the benefits of modern biblical studies but urges a closer working relationship between religious education and scholarly research.

20. One of the most important present-day developments along this line is feminist theological reflection upon women's experience. See, e.g., the American Academy of Religion 1981 presidential address of Jill Raitt, "Strictures and Structures: Relational Theology and a Woman's Contribution to Theological Conversation," *Journal of the American Academy of Religion* 50 (1982): 3–17.

21. Coleman, "The Two Pedagogies," pp. 58–61.

22. Ibid., p. 72.

4

Religious Education:
A Map of the Field

Mary C. Boys

There is a type of originality that breaks no rules, that produces
nothing radically new. Instead, the familiar world is seen from a
fresh angle; familiar elements are combined in a new way. This is
the originality of synthesis as distinct from the originality of exploration: Mozart rather than Beethoven.[1]

The sessions of the National Faculty Seminar that gave birth to
this volume involved lively discussion among scholars from
different fields committed to the mission of the church. Their
fields of study—Bible, philosophy of education, ethics, systematic theology, sociology of religion, and pastoral care—bear
directly on the way the church educates. But seminar members
asked the religious educators in the group: How do you understand religious education? In what way might religious education be considered a field in its own right? Wherein lies the
originality of religious education?

What follows is one way of thinking about religious education,
a *map* by which readers might situate themselves.[2] It represents
an attempt to (1) delineate some fundamental and perennial
questions that have shaped the field; (2) examine the way these
questions have been grappled with in particular contexts; and

(3) suggest the relation of present concerns—including these essays on the relation of citizenship and discipleship—to past ones.

A word of caution, however: maps, though useful, have their limits. As theoretical constructs, they offer a way of visualizing the territory, but maps are not the only way of describing the terrain. Consequently, the metaphor of map suggests that the way religious education is understood in this essay is not necessarily the way the field exists. Reality is always socially constructed.[3] Not only are there different ways of mapping the world (though we in North America are accustomed to seeing ourselves as front and center on most maps of the world), but studying a globe reminds us that the one-dimensional approach cannot capture everything. In addition, a map may be simultaneously accurate and deceptive, as anyone who has taken a map in hand to make his or her way through Boston soon realizes while wandering for miles on arterials "uncluttered" by any street signs. Descriptions may not always match realities.

In short, one's cartography is always shaped by standpoint, that is, by such factors as one's point of departure, mode of travel, and intended destination. Moreover, the cartographer's art, though important, is no substitute for on-site exploration.

Both points are vital to the essays of this volume insofar as they resulted from animated exchange among participants. Early on, members devoted one full session to a sort of autobiographical sharing, identifying and analyzing the effects of one's "social location" on scholarship and ecclesial commitment. In part, this was an attempt to identify some factors that condition the educational process and to acknowledge both the limited vantage point and distinct purview each scholar contributed. Consequently, the essays must be recognized as works shaped by their authors' assumptions, experiences, limitations, convictions, biases, and hopes—many beyond telling.

For instance, I sketch my map of the field of religious education as a post-Vatican II Catholic who has lived virtually all of her life in the United States in large cities of both the Pacific Northwest and the Northeast and who has never personally known real deprivation, either physical or psychological. It is a map constructed by one who sees reality through the critical lens of feminism; it is a map designed by one whose profession has always involved teaching and who is by vocation explicitly committed to educating in faith for the full development of the person. Furthermore, it is a perspective greatly limited by my relatively narrow field of experience. It shows only how one person, formed in a Western mind-set, understands what has been happening in Christian educational situations in the United States and Canada and is therefore reflective of only a very small part of this large and diverse planet.

Obviously, then, my attempt at cartography is only one possible way of describing the field of religious education. Other people, shaped by different standpoints, will offer alternative ways of laying out the field. But what is important is not so much that my categories become normative as that they provide a *historical perspective* and possibility of *common vocabulary.* Thus I hope to stimulate conversation across the disciplines and ultimately contribute to a deepening of understanding of how our activities of interpreting the Christian faith educate for the future good of the world.

My essay maps the field of religious education in a threefold framework. Initially, I lay out a basic guide for exploring—what I term "foundational questions." This section is analytical. Second, I do a survey of the territory—a historical tour of four "classic expressions" that represent the most significant avenues by which Protestants and Catholics have educated in faith in modern times in the West. Finally, I assume a "bird's-eye" view of new directions; it is in this section that I turn explicitly to the other essays in this volume.

I. A Basic Guide for Exploring:
Foundational Questions and Classic Expressions

Religious education is an ancient practice, yet a relatively young field. Every tradition has had its ways of handing on wisdom and knowledge in story, ritual, and explicit teaching, but efforts in recent years to clarify the dimensions of religious education indicate new intentionality.

This means that fundamental questions must be asked. Religious educators in the twentieth century cannot merely focus on the "how to?" ("How shall we convey God's revelation") but must inquire more deeply: "What does it mean to educate religiously?" The former question invites reductionism (religious education merely becomes a means of transmission), but the latter—the generating inquiry of my study—educes exploration of profound issues.

In the genesis of religious education as a distinct field (usually dated from the founding of the Religious Education Association in 1903),[4] a number of important books by such early leaders as George Albert Coe, Sophia Lyon Fahs, Josef Jungmann, and Johannes Hofinger established a rich agenda to which later generations of theorists insightfully contributed. In part, my task is to describe and order (albeit in exceedingly abbreviated form) what these theorists have proposed and thereby to sketch the contours of the field.

The concern for methodology has spawned another sort of effort: developing analytical categories for surveying the field. I think of such efforts as the typology developed by Jack L. Seymour;[5] John Elias's ordering of current theorists according to their predominant audience (public, academy, or church)[6] and especially of Harold Burgess's 1975 compendium, *An Invitation to Religious Education,* an inclusive review of the recent literature.[7] Each of these is a map of the field.

Yet my map will appear quite different from other typologies because I have found other categories more illuminating and a different division of schools of thought more representative of the history of the field. My construct consists of:

- foundational questions
- classic expressions and their contemporary modifications
- new developments and directions

Perhaps a few brief comments here on the entire panorama will suggest to the reader what view my logic affords.

My construct evolved from two thoughts that persisted in my attempts to teach the literature of twentieth-century religious education. The first involved the importance of history as the crucial context for interpretation, particularly since the first half of the twentieth century witnessed radically different rhythms in Protestantism and Catholicism. Thus, for instance, to include

Catholics such as Josef Jungmann and Johannes Hofinger with Protestant evangelicals such as Frank Gaebelein and Lois LeBar under the rubric of "traditional theological approach," as does Burgess, seriously obscures the dynamic of history as a context of theology.[8] Consequently, schools of thought I discerned— what I have termed "classic expressions"—needed to be historically situated. Moreover, I wanted to differentiate between their early development and the variations spawned in more recent years (especially from the late 1960s)—hence, "contemporary modifications." The second persistent notion revolved around certain questions that seemed to appear in differing guises and with varying degrees of explicitness and intensity but surfaced nonetheless in all the major schools of thought. These "foundational questions," each of which encompasses numerous other questions, seemed to me to constitute the most appropriately inclusive categories for analysis of each classic expression.

Two questions seemed to me to be so fundamental that they are obvious and yet (perhaps for that reason) easily overlooked: (1) What does it mean to be religious? (2) What does it mean to educate in faith, to educate persons to the religious dimensions of life? Specifying some of the most significant components of each question will enflesh each of these fundamental questions.

A. Foundational Questions

What Does It Mean to Be Religious?

"Religion" is a notoriously difficult term to define, and it is no less elusive in its adjectival form. Yet usage of the latter at least takes note of Wilfred Cantwell Smith's important caveat that one has fundamentally to do, not with *religions,* but with religious persons.[9] Thus the heart of this inquiry is discerning what the theorists in the various major approaches understood themselves to be doing when they sought to form persons as religious beings, that is, to lead people to both a deepened faith and a more adequate comprehension of it.

Numerous complex questions are intertwined in asking the more global question of what it means to be religious. The following five questions seem to undergird the classic expressions insofar as they have been addressed (at least implicitly) in assumptions, propositions, and practices particular to each.

How is God revealed? Wherein lies the fundamental locus of God's revelation? In scripture? in tradition? in experience? What is the significance of worship and prayer? Who is the God who reveals? What is the anthropology underlying the image of God?

What does it mean to be converted? Is one transformed for life at a particular moment or does conversion unfold gradually over one's lifetime? Is education to be directed toward conversion? If so, how and with what cautions toward the other's freedom? To what extent does conversion have a psychological component, and how much importance is to be given to psychology? How central is conversion in a theory of religious education?

What is faith? What is belief? How are faith and belief related? The distinction between faith, as one's primary apprehension of the sacred, and belief, as one's secondary, conceptual articulation of it, is frequently made today. But whether or not they have made explicit this distinction, how have religious educators seemed to understand their work in regard to forming people in faith and also to developing cognitive understandings? How important is assent to a creed? How important is cognition? How significant is the affective dimension of one's faith?

What is theology's role and significance? Just as faith and belief may be separated for the sake of analysis, so too may religion and theology. How is theology understood in each theory of religious education, and how important is it in the theory? What importance is given to the intellectual life?

What is the relation between religion and culture? Here the categories of H. Richard Niebuhr's classic, *Christ and Culture* (1951), are extremely useful.[10] Does one's commitment of faith lead to (1) an uncompromising countercultural stance? (2) an acquiescent position, receptive to the categories and claims of one's milieu and desirous of making one's faith "relevant" above all else? (3) a dualistic position, in which one acknowledges the essentially corrupt nature of humankind, yet recognizes both one's "caughtness" in it and God's sustaining grace? (4) a synthetic position, in which one sees God's rule established in the nature

of things and so attempts to reconcile divine and human into
one system? (5) a transformist position, in which one seeks to
change the world in accord with the values of one's faith?

The complexity of these questions obviously precludes simple
solutions; each could well lead to a lifetime of study. Their value
lies in their heuristic quality: *They function as leading questions, so
that we might discern in each of the classic expressions different ways of
understanding what it means to be religious.*

What Does It Mean to Educate in Faith?

Education, not unlike religion, is a frequently employed term
that varies widely in meaning. Again, when we list some of the
questions contained within the larger inquiry, the analytical
framework becomes clearer:

To what purposes does one educate another (or oneself)? What constitutes an educated person? Why does one educate in (or for)
faith: why not simply "be with" another person in faith? What is
encompassed by the term "education"?

What does it mean to know? to learn? How is knowing more than
comprehending information? What is the role of ritual, story,
and symbol? Can one always articulate or measure what has
been learned? What is the relation between knowledge and
know-how?

What is the role of the social sciences in religious education? How
much emphasis should be given to psychology, anthropology,
and sociology in developing a theory of religious education?
Within each, which field is stressed (e.g., developmental [either
structural or psychosocial] psychology, depth psychology, social
psychology, psychology of learning) and which theorists are
adhered to? How important is social science in relation to theology?

How shall we think of curriculum and teaching? What might a
curriculum developed from one of the classic expressions look
like? What is the teacher's role, and how significant is teaching
for religious education? What theories of curriculum and teaching undergird a particular theory?

In what way is education a political activity? Toward what view of
society is a theory of religious education oriented, either explicitly or implicitly? Can one find a "hidden" curriculum, that

is, those values conveyed by structures and procedures? Can one identify the components of a "null" curriculum, that is, what is taught by virtue of not being taught?

These ten questions (and their sub-questions) constitute the analytical categories for the classic expressions. Not all of the questions within are applicable to each classic expression, but they serve to delineate the basic thrust of the inquiry. At this point, they are somewhat abstract, but they will take on more concreteness when viewed in their historical manifestations.

B. Classic Expressions

Having clarified my understanding of "foundational questions," I turn now to stipulate my definition of "classic expressions." Simply put, I use that term to denote a specific, historical manifestation of educating in faith that has resulted from the intersection of a particular theological perspective with a particular educational outlook. In other words, my interest lies in identifying varying standpoints that have developed out of a combination of theological and educational understandings.

I have identified four classic expressions, although not without misgivings about terminology. One of the more troublesome terms is "religious education." As I develop below, historically speaking, religious education names a classic expression that represents the wedding of liberal theology and progressive education. Yet, only vaguely (if at all) related to its historical referent, it also denotes a synonym for "educating in faith." In order to keep the two usages distinct, I have chosen to italicize *religious education* whenever I refer to it as a classic expression; otherwise, it simply reflects a term I find to be an especially appropriate way of talking about educating in faith. For the sake of consistency, I have italicized each of the other three classic expressions; *evangelism, Christian education*, and *Catholic education/catechetics (catechesis)*.

II. Surveying the Territory

A. The Classic Expressions

Within the confines of my task for this essay I am choosing to report primarily the conclusions to which my historical interpretation has led. Thus, in this section I am admittedly painting with a broad stroke, omitting the rich detail of varying personalities and the dynamic of the exchange of ideas; narrative thereby gives way to analysis. But perhaps even this abbreviated version will demonstrate the usefulness of the foundational questions in giving some order to the field of religious education.

1. Evangelism

Of the classic approaches that have shaped contemporary religious education, *evangelism* is the most difficult to trace with precision. I find it necessary to stipulate a broad working definition: *preaching or teaching the scriptures in such a way as to arouse conversion.* Moreover, I understand revivalism and evangelicalism—which extended the revivalistic spirit and gave an urgency to mission—to constitute two closely linked manifestations of *evangelism.* I need to qualify this further: *evangelism* differs from the other classic expressions insofar as it is not primarily an educational model and, indeed, is usually linked more closely with preaching than teaching. Nevertheless, despite its relative lack of explicit attention to the educational agenda (though schooling was always important), *evangelism* has in fact been a powerfully formative means of educating in faith. It has, furthermore, largely established the agenda of American Protestant education in the twentieth century, since the classic expression *religious education* followed in its wake as its critique and *Christian education* in turn followed as an alternative to the liberal standpoint.

In evangelism it is quite evident that to be religious involves first and foremost recognizing the overwhelming importance of conversion, understood as a moment of decision to give oneself to Christ.[11] The God whom the scriptures revealed demanded the renunciation of one's sinful, evil ways; the threat of hell— fiercely preached by "pulpit artists"—was all too real if one did not heed God's commands. This understanding of revelation depended to a large degree on an anthropology rooted in the Calvinist conviction of humankind's innate depravity, although as revivalism developed, its Calvinism became obviously Arminian.

Of great significance in *evangelism* was what the first generation of revivalists termed "experimental faith." Precisely because
faith was a product of one's affections, of one's experiential
knowledge, belief (embodied in creeds and dogmas) played a
secondary role. Theology was not without significance, particularly to Jonathan Edwards and Charles Finney, but the con-
troversy in the First Great Awakening (1730–60) over what
constituted a "learned ministry" indicated the ever-present tensions exacerbated by the study of theology.

Yet even Gilbert Tennent, whose sermon on the converted
minister sparked that debate, had a high regard for education.
He, like nearly all the revivalists (excluding Dwight Moody and
Billy Sunday, for example), saw in education a means of deepening one's conversion. Tennent once concluded a sermon with a
reading list designed to guide the hearer toward conversion.
Essential to the early purposes of the revivalists was the creation
of "alternative education": "The public academies" are "so much
corrupted and abused generally" that "private schools or semi-
naries of learning which are under the care of skillful and experienced Christians" ought to be founded, argued Gilbert
Tennent.[12]

Educating religiously was inextricably linked to a view of
knowledge as *transformative:* mere rationality had no power to
lead to conversion. One learned in order to be changed from
depravity to grace. Consequently, as Lawrence Cremin percep-
tively notes, the revivalists did not in any fashion downplay
religious education—previously understood as memorization of
scripture, prayers, and the catechism—rather, they changed its
pedagogy: prophecy replaced edification as the central technique.[13] The schools were, after all, an adjunct to the church in
its "war on Satan." Yet ultimately the classical curriculum of the
academies and colleges served as a counterforce to the enthusiastic religion of the heart and thus functioned to give a more
humanistic orientation to American Protestantism.

Other organizations emerged in nineteenth-century evangelicalism to provide what Robert Wood Lynn has termed an
"ecology" of educational institutions which extended and deepened the conversions engendered in revivals.[14] These so-called
benevolent societies—the American Bible Society, American

Tract Society, Women's Christian Temperance Union, Home Missionary Society, American Peace Society, and American Anti-Slavery Society, among others—offered the nation a moral education, albeit also often a moralistic stewardship of the prosperous. Yet for all their shortcomings, these societies reflected a concern for the nation's values; they also significantly stimulated the participation of women in church life. Moreover, the mission orientation of evangelical women contributed vital energy and leadership to the suffrage movement.

In general, evangelism rested on a sharp distinction between natural and supernatural, secular and sacred. Yet its preachers and teachers most often could not recognize what a later age, with the benefit of hindsight, can recognize: they too were caught into certain cultural norms and beliefs, especially the "success ethic." Thus they generally failed to recognize the political nature of their educational activity and to examine how their exhortations shaped a people in the American mythology of the self-made person—a strange irony for a movement grounded, above all, in awareness of God's amazing grace.

2. Religious Education

Religious education names a classic expression that weds classic liberal theology and progressivist educational thought. Its boundaries, therefore, are easier to delineate and its theories more explicitly linked to the foundational questions. Yet it is more than a successor to the evangelistic impulse: *religious education* is both its alternative and its counterpoint. Just as *evangelism* had developed in reaction to the formalism and rationalism bequeathed to the churches by the Enlightenment, so did *religious education* have its genesis in opposition to many of the emphases of the revivalist preachers and of the benevolent societies.

Above all, the theorists of religious education manifested a deep faith in the steady unfolding of progress—for which evolution was a dominant metaphor—and in the power of education to reform society. John Dewey spoke of the teacher as a prophet and "usherer in" of God's reign; George Albert Coe (1862–1951), religious education's preeminent voice, fervently believed that education could change the church and, by so doing, "reconstruct" the world. Thus Coe regarded Jesus as the "Supreme Educator" and equated redemption with the process of education.

The commitments of Dewey and Coe to reconstructing the social order (a favorite phrase) meant that they understood the fundamental locus of God's revelation to be in the world, particularly in social interaction. Though they rejected neither the scriptures nor traditional forms of worship, they did not consider these as important as other Christians did. Coe disapproved of too much focus on the Bible, since he feared it would distract people from reality, and he regarded true worship as seeing life objectively.[15]

The theorists of *religious education* looked very critically at the way conversion was understood in *evangelism*, since it seemed to rest on an authoritarian God acting capriciously upon a passive creature. In contrast, they emphasized growth and continuity, substituting the educational process for conversion. Thus the vocabulary of nurture, formation, development, and wholeness assumed an ascendancy over discussion of sin and guilt.[16] Furthermore, conversion now became a subject of empirical study, and those who engaged in this research had often themselves undergone a sort of conversion to the methods of science.[17]

Their embrace of empiricism fostered a devaluation of the supernatural. As a consequence, adherence to a creed was looked upon as dogmatism and the educational process regarded as a necessary corrective of the indoctrinating ways of *evangelism*. Yet, despite their critical perspective on assent to traditional creedal formulations, Coe and his colleagues considered cognition to be extremely important. They had serious reservations about the enthusiasm unleashed by revivals and sought to counter this emotionalism with rational, analytical discussion. The affective dimension was not without its importance; Coe, for example, argued that "religious education must include provision for cultivating religious fervor."[18] Yet their commitment to scientific method entailed enormous respect for logic and critical thinking; ironically, theirs was often an enthusiastic appropriation of science, a passionate argument for rationality in religion.

For theology, however, they had little enthusiasm. Clearly, the theorists of *religious education* were decidedly uninterested in metaphysical questions and directed relatively little energy into theological debates.[19] The liberal theology upon which their assumptions rested exemplify Niebuhr's category of "Christ of culture," that is, a "culture Christianity" allied with self-reliant humanism. Conscious of their explicit commitment to reconstruction of the social order, leaders of the religious education movement equated education with salvation; moreover, they directed their concerns toward "the salvation of the world community" rather than merely the "salvation of a few select individuals."[20] Since they considered that there was no specifically "religious" subject matter, they designed curricula inclusive of a broad range of human concerns, a thematic particularly characteristic of Sophia Lyon Fahs.

Their epistemology provides some fascinating contrasts. On the one hand, the enthusiasm for empiricism reflected a tendency to quantify learning insofar as psychology developed along the (Edward) Thorndike trajectory, which rested on the assumption that one could measure learning and intelligence. Coe's early work on cases of conversion contributed to the establishment of the scientific study of religion, an endeavor that would have seemed bold to his evangelical predecessors, who would not have dared to presume to apply scientific categories to God's work in a person's soul. Of course, hindsight reveals the naiveté of the liberal-progressivist movement: the knowledge discovered by the "scientific method" is neither so objective nor so certain as its enthusiasts believed.

Yet, coexisting with this predilection for "objective" knowledge was a profound sense that true knowledge overflowed into action and was in turn changed by it. Dewey's aversion to dualism and his insistence upon the unity of theory and practice testified to this desire to understand knowledge as transformative. Coe's brilliance in illuminating the ethical foundation of spirituality likewise manifests a recognition that knowing far transcends mere comprehension. Moreover, fundamental to religious education was a commitment to "learn by doing" and thereby a rejection of the dichotomy between knowledge and know-how. This translated into a broadened notion of curriculum. For instance, Coe viewed the curriculum not simply as a structured progression of ideas or knowledge but as "an orderly succession of enterprises in and through which social appreciation, social habits, and social loyalties may grow into the full stature of the Christian faith."[21] "Learning by doing" also meant that the teacher's role primarily centered on design of activities and attention to facilitating growth; teachers needed to have skills in group process and a self-understanding as guides rather than as authoritarian figures.

The orientation toward learning through activity in part grew out of, and contributed to, the significant role of the social sciences in *religious education*. The emergence of a psychology of learning and of developmental psychology proved crucial to this classic expression; later, Freudian theory would influence progressive schools. Certainly the social sciences figured more prominently than did theology in the development of theory.

What the theorists of religious education made transparently clear was the political nature of education. "Hidden," of course, in their curriculum was the uncritical regard for democracy and the triumphalistic belief that progress was evolving steadily. What was given little emphasis, and tended to be a "null" curriculum, was traditional Christian doctrine.

As a classic expression, *religious education* reflects a radical departure both theologically and educationally from previous modes of educating in faith. The furor its radicality engendered energized the next movement: *Christian education.*

3. Christian Education

Simply put, to many the liberal-progressivist standpoint on educating in faith seemed to lack any distinctively Christian convictions—hence, *Christian education*, a theological critique of *religious education.*

The starting point for analysis of this classic expression is the question of the relation of religion and culture, since it was the neo-orthodox interpretation of the human situation that established its fundamental contours. The awareness of finitude and sinfulness, together with a sense of the transcendent God's gracious judgment, seemed to exemplify what H. Richard

Niebuhr termed the position of "Christ and culture in paradox," that sense of the whole edifice of culture being "cracked and madly askew" even while acknowledging God's sustaining power. This dualist position—a recognition of one's "caughtness" in a broken world and of one's utter dependence on grace—shaped a sharply theocentric outlook. The revelation of a transcendent God became a dominant theme, and this theme was played out in the distinctive emphases of the Biblical Theology Movement: God's progressive revelation in history, anticipated in the Old Testament, fulfilled in Jesus Christ, and continued in the life of the church. The scriptures played a central role in education, though not in a fundamentalist manner, since the new biblical theology incorporated many of the insights of the historical-critical method. Thus, much attention was devoted to the function of the Bible in the educational realm, a development most thoroughly analyzed by Sara Little.[22]

Assent to creedal formulations, moreover, assumed greater importance than heretofore; faith was seen as closely linked with classical statements of belief. Conversion was likewise regarded theologically, with little interest evidenced in psychological dynamics. Quite clearly, theology was viewed as the key constituent of *Christian education*, and the attention that was given to world religions, to psychology, and to sociology of religion by the proponents of *religious education* was dismissed as a turning away from the essentials of Christianity.

Thus theology, in the memorable phrase of Randolph Crump Miller, functioned as the "clue" to educating in faith.[23] Education generally played a less significant role: theology was the controlling partner.[24] In fact, the neo-orthodox critique of the liberals led to a suspicion of their entire educational stance as well. Thus, in Christian education, the activity method tended to be replaced by transmissive modes of teaching. The emphasis on God's revelatory word suggested a view of teaching as telling, as proclaiming "God's mighty acts." Virtually no attention was devoted to instilling "critical consciousness," and, though there was less naiveté about the nature of democracy, little emphasis was given to reforming the structures of society. Similarly, the dominance of theology resulted in less attention to the social sciences. Education was directed toward the formation of faithful followers of Jesus Christ; the focus was on an ecclesial rather than a worldly holiness.

Christian education had reactionary roots insofar as it represented the confluence of neo-orthodox theologies with an antiprogressivist educational outlook. Its characteristic stresses on proclaiming the word, divine transcendence, and divine authority in revelation took up and promulgated the emphases of the Biblical Theology Movement.[25] Though its theological premises dominated its conversation with education, *Christian education* quickly assumed a primary position among the mainline churches. Not until the late 1960s, when so many developments in the world led to new direction within the churches as well, did this classic expression undergo significant modification.

4. *Catholic Education/Catechetics*

This fourth classic expression reveals a distinctively Catholic approach to educating in faith; in addition, its compound name suggests a dual character. *Catholic education*, as Fayette Breaux Veverka has argued, might best be understood as a term expressive of a *paideia;* it mirrored a particular way of construing the relationship between religion and education that developed in the context of the alienation (both religious and cultural) of United States Catholic immigrants and also reflected the siege mentality of European-dominated, nineteenth-century Roman Catholicism. Though it came to expression in the Catholic school system, *Catholic education* embraced wider concerns about the relationship of faith to society and therefore should not merely be equated with Catholic schooling.[26]

Generally speaking, *Catholic education* prevailed as the most inclusive term until the years immediately following the Second Vatican Council (1962–65), when the term *catechetics* (alternatively, *catechesis*) emerged as the more dominant. *Catechetics* might be regarded as both a critique of the former and as a focusing or narrowing of the philosophy of Catholic education. Its twentieth-century origins lie with the so-called kerygmatic movement—a European renewal movement of the 1930s grounded in a return to biblical and liturgical roots and immensely influential in establishing the milieu for Vatican II. More recently, *catechetics* has become a term advocated by some

Roman Catholic and Protestant theorists as the most appropriate name for the broad range of activities involved in educating in faith.

The foundational questions provide a structure for reviewing the essence of *Catholic education*. Revelation was of first importance: God was revealed in the church (as the classic formula put it, *locutio Dei ad homines per modum magisterii*). The inheritance of Thomism meant a special emphasis on assent to truth, since for Aquinas revelation was the saving act by which God gave humankind the truths necessary for salvation. Faith enabled believers to assent to the divine truths, which were given expression in the church's creeds. Thus, adherence to the church's teaching was seen as the primary mode of acceptance of God's revelation. To know meant to give assent to truth expressed in propositional form.

As Niebuhr has shown, classical Thomistic thought offered a synthesist position on Christ and culture: God's rule was shown to be established in the nature of things, and salvation did not entail the destruction of the created order, since grace is built upon nature. This synthesist perspective, however, came to coexist with a more negative assessment of culture. As the church dealt with the political, social, and economic realities of the nineteenth century, it became increasingly defensive toward the wider culture and seemed to withdraw itself from the world. Thus, *Catholic education* had a Janus-like quality: on the one hand, it prized culture and learning, and proclaimed that "nothing human was alien"; on the other, it looked severely on the Enlightenment's motto (from Kant), "Dare to think for yourself," and condemned modernity. This paradox is at least partially explained in Langdon Gilkey's distinction that Catholicism had long honored speculative reason but that its ecclesiology fostered a negative judgment of critical reason.[27]

Philosophy and theology were regarded as the epitome of human knowledge and undergirded the understanding of education; they also served as principles by which one could criticize the social sciences. The church regarded education as of supreme importance because it involved the formation of the whole person; education was one of the prime means by which persons developed Christian character and, thereby, prepared themselves for heaven. It was, significantly, a "permeation theory": Catholic educational philosophy embraced the whole of a person's life. At its best, *Catholic education* "represented a public vision of religious education that understood that education was broader than schooling and that religion was broader than church or creed."[28] Yet its assumptions were grounded in a worldview that could no longer be sustained once Catholicism truly wrestled with modernity rather than simply condemned it. Thus it was that Vatican II—the Catholic Church's long-delayed confrontation with the modern era—led inevitably to a reconsideration of what it means to educate in faith. The absolutist and ahistorical basis of *Catholic education* could not hold, though its holistic emphases were in a genuine way prophetic.

The ferment in thought that ultimately came to expression in Vatican II—most particularly in the "Constitution on the Sacred Liturgy" (*Sacrosanctum concilium*) and in the "Dogmatic Constitution on Divine Revelation" (*Dei verbum*)—profoundly shaped the emphases of *catechetics*. The new vigor with which the Catholic Church took up the study of scripture, and its recognition of the unity of scripture and tradition, meant that *catechetics* must necessarily be biblically grounded. Its categorization as a form of ministry of the word revealed its inherent linkage with liturgical life, certainly one of the most singular characteristics of *catechetics*.

The intimate bond between liturgy and *catechetics* has given rise to new perspectives on conversion, which has been seen in more recent years as a countercultural realignment of one's values in accordance with the words and deeds of Jesus—or, in a word, as the essence of *discipleship*. The task of *catechetics*, therefore, is to deepen conversion so that people can better discern God's ways in the social sphere and thus participate in the church's prophetic mission.

Implicit here is a sense of the church's ambiguous relation with culture. Unlike the world-condemning, turn-of-the-century documents of the Modernist crisis, the documents of Vatican II expressed an awareness of the goodness of all creation. Yet within those same documents—and indeed in a series of subsequent documents such as Pope Paul VI's encyclical of 1967, *Populorum progressio*, and the 1971 Synod's *Justice in the World*—

the Catholic Church has at the same time recognized the prevalence of sinful social structures. In Niebuhrian terms, what seemed to be emerging from the post-Vatican II church was a transformist position, in which the values engendered by faith served as the basis for making societal changes. The emergence of *catechetics* represented a more complex perspective on the church's role in the world.

Another tension inherent in *catechetics* centers on the relationship between faith and belief. Whereas previously faith had been regarded primarily in intellectualist terms as an illumination of the soul that implied adherence to a body of propositional truths, now it took on a more existential character. Faith frequently came to be spoken of as summoning the adherence of the whole person and as linked with one's process of maturing. At the same time, there is the faith *which* one believes, that is, faith as expressed in creeds, dogmas, moral principles, and doctrine. To call people to mature in faith as they deepen in adherence to the community's professed faith has in practice meant at numerous junctures considerable tension between forces desiring more attention to the church's official teaching and those who have devoted less attention to doctrine in their attempt to foster a personal life of faith.

Despite differences that exist on the relation of faith and belief, all catechetical theorists place great importance on theology. There appears to be a discomfort with educational language, lest *catechetics* seem to be too closely linked with schooling and, consequently, betray an excessively cognitive end. Catechetical theory in general has given little sustained attention to matters of curriculum and teaching. As in *Christian education*, theology dominates the conversation with education.

The question of the role and significance of the social sciences, however, has increasingly become of vital importance. The usage of a phrase such as "maturity of faith" in the U.S. National Catechetical Directory, *Sharing the Light of Faith*, signals a receptivity to developmental psychology, and its opening chapter, which seeks to describe the specific cultural and religious characteristics that affect educating in faith in the United States, gives evidence of increased attention to sociology, though not of a sociology of knowledge.

But what seems to be missing in catechetical theory—and herein lies a clue to education as a political activity—is any sense of critical ecclesiology. Contemporary *catechetics* seems fundamentally to be concerned with the process of socialization into the believing community. For that reason, among others, a number of critics (of whom I am one) claim that it is not an adequate theory upon which to base one's entire understanding of what it means to educate in faith.

B. Contemporary Modifications of the Classic Expressions

In this section and the one that follows, I shall deal very briefly and selectively with the classic expressions in their current status. I wish at this juncture simply to show the broad outlines of the trajectories the four classic expressions assumed in the late 1960s to the present.

1. Evangelism

The spectrum of contemporary evangelical life has hues of many colors, and its fascinating mosaic serves as a warning against simplistic generalizations. Because the differences tend to cluster around varying judgments on the nature of scriptural revelation (especially on inerrancy) and on social ethics (especially on the question of Christ and culture), theology provides a useful analytic framework. But when educational philosophy is also taken into account, then three patterns seem to develop: (a) Christian education as transmission of the truth, as illustrated in "the electronic church" and in Christian academies;[29] (b) Christian education as faith shared in a countercultural, apostolic community, as evidenced in the journalistic endeavors and witness of the Sojourners Fellowship (an intentional Christian community that works for justice and publishes the monthly journal *Sojourners*); and (c) religious education as mission energized by the fellowship of congregational life, as manifest in the mainline evangelical churches. Only from the latter has there been explicit attention to the nature and function of educating in faith.[30] And, as different as are the "electronic church" preachers and the Sojourners Fellowship members, both consider citizenship to be integrally related to discipleship—though they disagree on the particulars of this relation.

2. Religious Education

Each of the classic expressions is a mosaic, bringing together various elements into the harmony of one design. *Religious education*, for instance, encompassed William Channing's Unitarianism, Horace Bushnell's preference for nurture within the family over adolescent conversion, and the Dewey-Coe-Elliott commitment to education as reconstruction. These elements have continued through to the present day in the educational commitments of the Unitarian Universalist Church and its "cousin" traditions, such as the Ethical Culture Society; in the work of the Religious Research Unit at Manchester College, Oxford;[31] and in the work of theorists Paulo Freire and Gabriel Moran. What is shared by all of these is a strong conviction about the centrality of one's public role as a disciple.

3. Christian Education

Perhaps the chief characteristic of *Christian education* in its classic mode was the significant role assigned to theology, particularly biblical theology. As the Biblical Theology Movement declined in the wake of developments in historical criticism and "postcritical" biblical study, the neo-orthodox categories that had dominated became less influential. Thus, for instance, Randolph Crump Miller sought to bring the categories of process theology to bear on religious education[32] and modified his earlier position: theology and educational theory must have equal voice in religious education.[33] C. Ellis Nelson, drawing upon different perspectives from the various New Testament communities in *Where Faith Begins*, showed that the congregation's life itself constitutes a curriculum, and so integrated cultural anthropology and sociology to develop his thesis that the meaning of faith is developed by the congregation's members out of their history and mutual interactions in relation to events taking place in their lives.[34] In short, the dialectical theology that had characterized the classic form of *Christian education* has been replaced by other theological perspectives, and greater appropriation is made of the social sciences.

Christian education remains today the dominant terminology and reflects a variety of theological and educational views not necessarily indebted to the Barthians—as its increased usage among Roman Catholics signals.[35] Its broadened theological base and its openness to the social sciences suggest the adaptability of this modified classic expression.[36] These same characteristics also help to account for a certain lack of clarity about its nature and purpose.

4. Catholic Education/Catechetics

Though in many respects *Catholic education* has become virtually synonymous with Catholic schools, its permeation theory is gradually being reformulated on the basis of more adequate assumptions. One example of this reconsideration is the pastoral letter of the American bishops, *To Teach as Jesus Did*, in which the educational mission of the church is spoken of as an "integrated ministry embracing three interlocking dimensions: the message revealed by God (*didachē*) which the church proclaims; fellowship in the life of the Holy Spirit (*koinōnia*); service to the Christian community and the entire human community (*diakonia*)."[37] Significantly, what this document also recognizes is that the continuing education of adults is at the center of the church's educational mission. This constitutes a major shift in emphasis, as previously the church's educational resources had been devoted almost exclusively to its young. In practice, this has frequently meant Catholic schools vying for funds with other educative agencies in the parish.

The importance given to the education of adults is likewise evident in the heralded *Rite of Christian Initiation of Adults* (RCIA), a 1972 revision of the rite of adult baptism modeled upon the catechumenate of the early church. The liturgists have taken the lead here and seem to be hesitant to work under the rubric of "education," lest that field be too didactic and cognitive for the sort of conversion they envision; thus, catechetical language prevails. Interestingly, many think of the RCIA as the process most capable of renewing the church. It, however, is a conversation, as Brueggemann might have expressed it, that takes place almost entirely "behind the wall." The RCIA is a formation program: participants are meant to tap into the "energizing symbols" and "primal language" of the community of faith.[38]

III. New Developments and Directions: A Bird's-Eye View

Again, this section will be brief, since the purpose is merely to indicate some of the developments and directions that, though not unrelated to the classic expressions, nonetheless reflect emphases not always congruent with their overall pattern; they are also indicative of the kaleidoscopic character of contemporary religious education. I will, in addition, indicate some points of convergence with the other essays in this volume.

1. Role of the Affections and of the Nondiscursive

Sorting out the appropriate role of the emotions in educating in faith has long been a controversial issue, often exciting passionate countercharges of "uninspired" or "enthusiastic." At issue is the question of what it means for a person of faith to know; grappling with the questions that cluster around that inquiry involves exploring the ways in which worship shapes a person's (and a community's) commitment, and the role of the aesthetic in teaching that form of knowledge which is tacit and nondiscursive. Among religious educators working in these areas are John H. Westerhoff III (in collaboration with anthropologist Gwen Kennedy Neville)[39]; and Maria Harris, Gloria Durka, and Joanmarie Smith.[40] Also related here is the increased attention to the role of narrative and story.

Karen Lebacqz offers a related point in her argument that critical rationality is insufficient for learning ethics: one must supplement research and analysis with the deeper and more painful reality of acknowledging one's own participation in oppression.[41]

2. Role of the Social Sciences

Here three distinct emphases are clear: (a) a predilection for developmental psychology revealed in the significance granted to the stage theories of Lawrence Kohlberg and James Fowler;[42] (b) a turning toward theories of adult education;[43] and (c) an advocacy of a theory of religious education undergirded by social science rather than by theology.[44]

To engage in religious education today means confronting the proper role of the social sciences, a concern Don Browning raises in his charge that, because Christian religious education has been inadequately anchored in the fundamental discipline of practical theology, many of its practitioners have made an un-critical use of various social sciences.[45]

3. Role of Theology

Though some—most notably Don Browning in his elaborately argued essay in this volume—would subsume religious educa-tion under practical theology,[46] other theorists in the field resist such a classification. Two reasons seem to be operative in this resistance. The first centers around an attempt to pay greater heed to the religious character of people's lives and thus to appropriate more consciously ways of deepening their apprecia-tion of mystery and paradox before utilizing the secondary language of theology. The second emerges from a concern to integrate educational philosophy into theories of religious edu-cation.[47] It is with this viewpoint I sympathize, as too often theology dominates the conversation with education, a situation that leads, ironically, to educational faddism. Nevertheless, I believe that Browning's argument about the necessity of deepen-ing educators' grasp of theological ethics is an astute and impor-tant one.

Moreover, the debate about theology's role ought not to obscure the obligation of religious educators to teach an ade-quate understanding of Christianity. Particularly valuable, then, is the proposal of Bernard Cooke that Christians, while not needing extensive or technical knowledge, must have *some* fun-damental understandings.[48] One's religious commitments are vitally affected by one's theological knowledge; as Cooke ob-serves, there are certain basics that "people need in order to deal religiously with the experienced reality of their human life."[49]

4. The Public Character

One very important development in religious education is a new sense of the public obligation of religious education—that is, for people within religious traditions to speak a language understandable to those outside the traditions. Gabriel Moran has been the theorist in the field most insistent on this matter,[50] and his arguments take on a new force when read in tandem with Martin Marty's *The Public Church* and Parker Palmer's *The Company of Strangers*. More recently, a team of religious educators has called for enhancing the church's participation in the education of the public.[51]

It is in this area that many of the concerns of the National Faculty Seminar surface, and certainly here the themes of this volume are most obvious. John Coleman's argument that responsible citizenship enhances one's practice of discipleship because it offers a wider solidarity, a humbler service, and a more taxing "reality test" offers religious educators a challenge to develop more adequate ways of grasping the political import of Christian commitment.[52]

Walter Brueggemann, although also cognizant of the church's obligation to nurture people's bilinguality (communal and public languages), maintains that it must first and foremost teach a sectarian hermeneutic as the source of the community's identity, energy, and power. Only, he asserts, the language of "transformative imagination"—the speech of faithful believers—will prevent the language of "policy formation" from becoming the ideology of the empire.[53]

One may discern in the essays of Coleman and Brueggemann differing ways of locating the church in the world. Religious educators following Brueggemann's lead would give virtually no attention to the education of the public; rather, their focus would be on forming people in the sectarian hermeneutic so that the church could challenge the world. Those influenced by Coleman would give more attention to what is sometimes termed "education for social responsibility." They would educate for a vocation in which people's calling is "to construct—using only the political materials we human beings have at hand—at least an approximation of that undistorted communication in neighbor love envisioned by God's new community."[54] While I do not wish to drive a wedge between these two essays, I think educators in the church will need to weigh their respective emphases and consider precisely how each would shape the curriculum—and with what significance for the church in the world.

One who wishes to inquire further into the complexities of religious education and the public should study the companion volume, which is a case study of the way one congregation made a decision about citizenship and discipleship.[55]

5. Reconstructing the Transformative Character

Among the most influential developments in the field of religious education in the past fifteen years has been the appropriation of liberation themes. Especially since the publication in English of Paulo Freire's *Pedagogy of the Oppressed* in 1970 (originally published in Portuguese, 1968), many religious educators have been preoccupied by a commitment to pass on the faith in such a way that the social order is changed. Foremost have been Thomas H. Groome's "shared praxis" approach and Letty Russell's attempt to formulate a "pedagogy for oppressors" and a "curriculum of subversion."[56] At the root of these pedagogies is a "critical consciousness," a term that implies, among other realities, a deep suspicion of what are regarded as the taken-for-granted realities.

Russell's work in particular offers some help to Karen Lebacqz, who asks about educating oppressors.[57] Russell proposes the usefulness of a "curriculum of subversion." This curriculum has three major components: (1) thinking from the other end (trying to take on another's more prophetic way of looking at things), (2) acting for social change, and (3) learning to think critically. Moreover, Russell offers three clues for helping oppressors become partners: (1) thinking from the other side, including transferring one's own experience of victimization and alienation to that of the experience of others; (2) loving the questions; and (3) identifying with the marginalized, that is, learning to sit where others sit.[58] Although Russell does not explicitly utilize pain as a category in her pedagogy, her curriculum of subversion inevitably involves it.

Conclusions

What does this cartographer see after her journey? Let me briefly draw a few conclusions and propose a definition of religious education.

First, the field of religious education has certain issues that are so vital and so complex that no one theory or school of theorists can ever satisfactorily resolve them. We need especially to know our history, so that we can get a perspective on our own standpoints.

Second, I believe that we need to think of the field in ways that are broadly inclusive, so as to honor the diverse ways men and women in different cultures and religious traditions have sought to educate in faith. A definition of the field should take into account the differences in theology and educational theory.

Accordingly, I advocate the following definition of the field: *Religious education is the making accessible of the traditions of the religious community and the making manifest of the intrinsic linkage between traditions and transformation.*

This definition entails understanding one's traditions as mediated in songs, social institutions, moral codes, myths, and dance patterns, as well as in scriptures, creeds, and theological formulations. It means seeing the traditions in their historical context and wrestling with their diversity and contradictions. The definition further entails conceptualizing teaching as an art of disciplined imagination that functions as a critical hermeneutic in communities of faith. To "give access" to traditions implies not only deep knowledge of traditions but also an interpretative framework drawn from the community.[59] Furthermore, it means seeking to show forth the traditions in as luminous a manner as possible, which implies the exercise of creativity. In my judgment, far too little attention in our field has been devoted to the art of teaching (which can only be learned by praxis). Sara Little's *To Set One's Heart* is a much-needed contribution.[60]

My definition also implies the commitment to make transparent the implications of traditions. Traditions are for the sake of changing the religious community and world, not for shoring up the status quo. But if the individual conscience is to be respected, then those who educate in faith must restrict themselves to *showing* the connections, not to *imposing* them upon the community. This implies the primacy of dialogical education. In Bernard Lonergan's terms, it seems to mean that the religious educator's task is oriented primarily toward intellectual conversion—or, as Karen Lebacqz might put it, appropriating the challenging teachings of Jesus, so as to lead people to that inevitably painful "sea change" we call conversion.

Religious education is a field in which familiar elements are combined in a new way. Its originality is indeed that of synthesis. Those who seek to understand it must work in partnership with other specialists in interpreting the Christian tradition so as to educate for the future good of the world.

NOTES

1. John Anthony West, review of *Ceremonial Time* by John Hanson Mitchell, *New York Times Book Review,* 12 August 1984, p. 27.

2. "All theory may be regarded as a kind of map extended over space and time" (Michael Polanyi, *Personal Knowledge: Towards a Post-Critical Philosophy* [New York: Harper & Row, Harper Torchbooks, 1964], p. 4). The map I outline in this essay is detailed at length in my *Educating in Faith: Maps and Visions* (San Francisco: Harper & Row, 1989).

3. See Peter L. Berger and Thomas Luckmann, *The Social Construction of Reality: A Treatise in the Sociology of Knowledge* (Garden City, N.Y.: Doubleday & Co., 1966).

4. See Stephen A. Schmidt, *A History of the Religious Education Association* (Birmingham, Ala.: Religious Education Press, 1983). Though from its earliest days, the Association had Jewish membership (p. 34) and articles by Jews occur with relative frequency in its journal, *Religious Education,* to date Jews have not participated actively in the debate over methodological concerns. I very much regret my exclusion of Jewish literature in this survey, but the lack of symmetry in categories and concerns has made inclusion too difficult.

5. Jack L. Seymour, "Contemporary Approaches to Christian Education," *Chicago Theological Seminary Bulletin* 69 (1979): 1–10.

6. John Elias, "The Three Publics of Religious Educators," *Religious Education* 77 (1982): 615–27. Elias, of course, is extrapolating from the work of David Tracy, *The Analogical Imagination: Christian Theology and the Culture of Pluralism* (New York: Crossroad, 1981), pp. 3–46.

7. Harold W. Burgess, *An Invitation to Religious Education* (Birmingham, Ala.: Religious Education Press, 1975).

126 MARY C. BOYS

8. Burgess, *Invitation*, pp. 21–58.

9. Wilfred Cantwell Smith, *The Meaning and End of Religion* (San Francisco: Harper & Row, 1978), p. 153.

10. H. Richard Niebuhr, *Christ and Culture* (New York: Harper & Brothers, 1951).

11. In the Catholic tradition, this view of conversion was manifest in the parish missions, although the moment of decision was framed in terms of a return to the sacraments. See Jay P. Dolan, *Catholic Revivalism: The American Experience, 1830–1900* (Notre Dame, Ind.: University of Notre Dame Press, 1978).

12. Cited in Douglas Sloan, *The Great Awakening and American Education: A Documentary History* (New York: Teachers College Press, 1973), p. 100.

13. Lawrence Cremin, *American Education: The Colonial Experience, 1607–1783* (New York: Harper & Row, 1970), p. 321.

14. Robert Wood Lynn, "Sometimes on Sunday: Reflections on Images of the Future in American Education," *Andover Newton Quarterly* 12 (1972): 130–39.

15. During a capital-labor conflict in the Kentucky coal mines, Coe remarked: "O ye metaphysicians! If there be a God, he is in Harlan County, Kentucky. Show us him, that we may worship! If you cannot find him in Harlan County, your talk about the universe in general will not bring us to our knees" (cited in H. Shelton Smith, "George Albert Coe, Revaluer of Values," *Religion in Life* 22 [1952–53]: 55).

16. As was the case among most liberals, the confidence in progress (including the notion of "progressive revelation") and in God's immanence meant a definite deemphasis on sin and guilt. But for the most perceptive and thorough statement from an advocate of *religious education*, see Harrison S. Elliott, *Can Religious Education Be Christian?* (1940; reprint, New York: Macmillan Co., 1949), pp. 140–97.

17. George Albert Coe wrote of his own "conversion" as a young man: "I settled the question, as far as I was concerned, on a Sunday morning by solemnly espousing the scientific method, including it within my religion, and resolving to follow it wherever it should lead" ("My Own Little Theatre," in *Religion in Transition*, ed. Vergilius T. Ferm [New York: Macmillan Co., 1937], p. 95). Later he wrote, "I judge that the most significant turning point in my life, religiously considered, was this early turning away from dogmatic method to scientific method" ("My Search for What Is Most Worthwhile," *Religious Education* 47 [1952]: 176).

18. George Albert Coe, *A Social Theory of Religious Education* (New York: Charles Scribner's Sons, 1917; reprint, New York: Arno Press, 1969), p. 340.

19. Elliott acknowledged the validity of the criticism that *religious*

education did not have an adequate metaphysical grounding (Elliott, *Can Religious Education Be Christian?* p. 267).

20. Sophia Lyon Fahs, *Today's Children and Yesterday's Heritage* (Boston: Beacon Press, 1952), p. 152.

21. Coe, *Social Theory,* p. 81.

22. Sara Little, *The Role of the Bible in Contemporary Christian Education* (Richmond: John Knox Press, 1961).

23. Randolph Crump Miller, *The Clue to Christian Education* (New York: Charles Scribner's Sons, 1950), p. 15. See his earlier comment (1943): "Someone has to make a Christian out of John Dewey" (cited in Randolph Crump Miller, "Theology in the Background," in *Religious Education and Theology,* ed. Norma H. Thompson, [Birmingham, Ala.: Religous Education Press, 1982], p. 21).

24. An exception might be D. Campbell Wyckoff; see his book, *The Gospel and Christian Education* (Philadelphia: Westminster Press, 1959).

25. One of the premier Old Testament scholars of the day, James D. Smart, wrote on *Christian education* (see particularly his *The Teaching Ministry of the Church* [Philadelphia: Westminster Press, 1954]) and served as the major author of the influential Faith and Life Curriculum for the United Presbyterian Church, U.S.A.

26. Fayette Breaux Veverka, "Defining a Catholic Approach to Education in the United States, 1920–1950" (Paper presented to the Association of Professors and Researchers in Religious Education, Anaheim, California, 19 November 1983).

27. Langdon Gilkey, *Catholicism Confronts Modernity: A Protestant View* (New York: Seabury Press, 1975), p. 23.

28. Veverka, "Defining a Catholic Approach," p. 32.

29. See Alan Peshkin's incisive analysis, *God's Choice: The Total World of a Fundamentalist Christian School* (Chicago: University of Chicago Press, 1986).

30. See especially Lawrence O. Richards, *A Theology of Christian Education* (Grand Rapids, Mich.: Zondervan Publishing House, 1975). The theorists in the evangelical tradition now generally use the term *Christian education.*

31. The Religious Education Research Unit was founded by Sir Alister Hardy in 1969 to challenge scientists to give proper recognition to the role of religious experience in human life. See the work of the present director, Edward Robinson, *The Original Vision: A Study of the Religious Experience of Childhood* (New York: Seabury Press, 1983).

32. See Randolph Crump Miller, *The Theory of Christian Education Practice: How Theology Affects Christian Education* (Birmingham, Ala.: Religious Education Press, 1980), pp. 22–46.

33. Miller, "Theology in the Background," in Thompson, *Religious Education,* p. 31.

128   MARY C. BOYS

34. C. Ellis Nelson, *Where Faith Begins* (Atlanta: John Knox Press, 1967).

35. Most notably in Thomas H. Groome, *Christian Religious Education: Sharing Our Story and Vision* (San Francisco: Harper & Row, 1980).

36. See especially Craig Dykstra, *Vision and Character: A Christian Educator's Alternative to Kohlberg* (New York: Paulist Press, 1981); Mary Elizabeth Moore, *Education for Continuity and Change: A New Model for Christian Religious Education* (Nashville: Abingdon Press, 1983); and Sara Little, *To Set One's Heart: Belief and Teaching in the Church* (Atlanta: John Knox Press, 1983).

37. *To Teach as Jesus Did* (Washington, D.C.: United States Catholic Conference, 1973).

38. See, in this volume, Walter Brueggemann, "The Legitimacy of a Sectarian Hermeneutic: 2 Kings 18—19," pp. 12, 28.

39. John H. Westerhoff III and Gwen Kennedy Neville, *Learning Through Liturgy* (New York: Crossroad, 1978).

40. Gloria Durka and Joanmarie Smith, eds., *Aesthetic Dimensions of Religious Education* (New York: Paulist Press, 1979).

41. See, in this volume, Karen Lebacqz, "Pain and Pedagogy: A Modest Proposal," esp. pp. 165–70.

42. These stage theories have dominated the literature in recent years. For critique, see Dykstra, *Vision and Character*; and Gabriel Moran, *Religious Education Development: Images for the Future* (Minneapolis, Minn.: Winston Press, 1983).

43. See Leon McKenzie, *The Religious Education of Adults* (Birmingham, Ala.: Religious Education Press, 1982).

44. This has been the agenda of James Michael Lee. See his trilogy: *The Shape of Religious Instruction* (Dayton: Pflaum, 1971); *The Flow of Religious Instruction* (Dayton: Pflaum, 1973); and *The Content of Religious Instruction* (Birmingham, Ala.: Religious Education Press, 1985).

45. See, in this volume, Don Browning, "Religious Education as Growth in Practical Theological Reflection and Action," pp. 137–39.

46. Ibid.

47. See Mary C. Boys, "The Role of Theology in Religious Education," *Horizons* 11 (1984): 61–85.

48. See, in this volume, Bernard Cooke, "Basic Christian Understandings."

49. Ibid., pp. 80–81.

50. See Gabriel Moran, *The Present Revelation: The Search for Religious Foundations* (New York: Herder & Herder, 1972); and idem, *Religious Body: Design for a New Reformation* (New York: Seabury Press, 1974).

51. Jack L. Seymour, Robert T. O'Gorman, and Charles R. Foster, *The*

Church in the Education of the Public: Refocusing the Task of Religious Education (Nashville: Abingdon Press, 1984).

52. See, in this volume, John A. Coleman, "The Two Pedagogies: Discipleship and Citizenship," pp. 59–61. See also his *An American Strategic Theology* (New York: Paulist Press, 1982).

53. See Brueggemann, "The Legitimacy of a Sectarian Hermeneutic," p. 28.

54. Coleman, "The Two Pedagogies: Discipleship and Citizenship," p. 62.

55. Nelle G. Slater, ed., *Tensions Between Citizenship and Discipleship: A Case Study* (New York: Pilgrim Press, 1989).

56. Groome, *Christian Religious Education;* and Letty Russell, *Growth in Partnership* (Philadelphia: Westminster Press, 1971). Note Groome's influence on Browning.

57. See Lebacqz, "Pain and Pedagogy."

58. Russell, *Growth in Partnership,* pp. 127–34.

59. See C. Ellis Nelson, "The Role of Teaching Within the Church," in Slater, *Tensions.*

60. Little, *To Set One's Heart.* See also my review of the literature, "Teaching: The Heart of Religious Education," *Religious Education* 79 (1984): 252–72.

PART III

Implications for Theological Education

5

Religious Education as Growth in Practical Theological Reflection and Action

Don S. Browning

CHRISTIAN RELIGIOUS EDUCATION should be conceived and ordered as an aspect of practical theology. Doing this will not only clarify the place of Christian religious education within the curriculum of theological education, it will also illuminate the very process, dynamics, and aims of Christian religious education itself. Christian religious education should be understood as a process of practical theology aimed at creating individuals capable of entering into a community of theological reflection and participating in the action that will follow from it. Accordingly, I will argue that Christian religious education ought to be guided by a model of practical theology employing the "revised correlational method," which, among its other aspects, assigns a prominent role to theological ethics. After describing the way three Christian educators utilize practical theology in their theories, I will elaborate on my own proposal. My theory assigns particular emphasis to the correlation between the ethics of principle and the ethics of character. Moreover, I delineate five dimensions of practical moral thinking that I maintain are fundamental to the enterprise of Christian education.

The Method of Practical Theology:
A Revised Correlational Model

The phrase "revised correlational model" refers to a distinctive approach to theology associated with the name of David Tracy. Tracy's sources are multiple, but as applied to practical theology, something like Tracy's methodology was developed in the writings of Seward Hiltner and Daniel Day Williams, although there is no evidence that Tracy himself has in any way relied on these two thinkers.[1]

In a variety of recent writings I have outlined my own views as to what this method would look like when applied to practical theology. Tracy's writings have applied the method primarily to fundamental and systematic theology,[2] although he has indeed said some very important things about practical theology, and this promises to be the next subject of his major three-volume work on theology.

In the pages below, I loosely follow Tracy, while developing some of his insights in directions suitable to my own position as recently set forth in my *Religious Ethics and Pastoral Care* (1983).[3] The revised correlational model is somewhat different from the widely used correlational model advocated by the late Paul Tillich. Tillich's method was primarily a matter of correlating existential questions derived from an analysis of ordinary cultural and personal experience. The answers to these questions, he believed, could be found in the Christian revelation. A revised correlational method, on the other hand, attempts to correlate both the questions and the answers about human existence, derived from an interpretation of the central Christian witness, *with* the questions and answers implicit in various interpretations of ordinary human experience.

The same method applied to practical theology means a critical correlation between the norms for human action and fulfillment revealed in interpretations of the Christian witness *with* the norms for action and fulfillment implicit in various interpretations of ordinary human experience. At the outset, it should be noticed that the method of revised correlation deals with *interpretations*—interpretations of the norms of action and fulfillment to be found in the Christian witness and in ordinary experience. I emphasize interpretations because the practical theologian never has access to either the raw uninterpreted Christian fact or the unbiased and uninterpreted reality of ordinary experience. This is why practical theology must be seen, as should Christian religious education, as an interpretative or hermeneutical task.

The revised correlational method is particularly powerful for clarifying the relation of discipleship and citizenship, the major themes of these essays. Insofar as practitioners of the revised correlational method are interested in interpretations of the central Christian witness, they are interested in clarifying the meaning of discipleship. Theologians who use the revised correlational method begin by taking an insider's view of the self-interpretation of the Christian faith and what it means for the Christian life, that is, discipleship. They are interested in the Christian church's self-interpretation of the meaning of Jesus as the Christ and what it means to live a life in which Christ is the primary influence and guide. But their use of the revised correlational method is, I believe, most fruitful in clarifying the meaning of citizenship and the relation of discipleship to the category of citizenship, especially in their ability to illuminate the relation of discipleship to the public world—the world of citizenship. Practitioners of the revised correlational method clarify the realms of overlapping truth that may exist between Christianity and the pluralism of faiths which besets public life in advanced societies.

Theologians who use the revised correlational approach assume that God works in creation and history both within and outside the manifest church. For this reason, theologians are searching to clarify points of conflict and uncover points of identity between the primary tradition that they represent and the other traditions that impinge upon their social worlds. Based upon this theological premise about God's relation to the world, they assume that the possible correlations between the central Christian witness and ordinary cultural and personal experience can be a matter of either identity, complete difference, or analogy.

For instance, a particular interpretation of the Christian witness and a particular interpretation of cultural experience can appear to be in such agreement as to be almost identical, at least on certain points. Or these two perspectives might appear to be in total disagreement and be absolutely different. Here the correlation would be virtually negative or zero.

But then, and this is what most generally happens, the correlation may be primarily a matter of analogy. When this happens, the Christian witness and the cultural witness look very much alike on certain matters but yet are still somewhat different. The analogical relation which sometimes occurs becomes very important for the purposes of practical theology. When analogy occurs, the Christian witness and various cultural perspectives can join together in common citizenship to create a public world.

The value of the revised correlational method is its basis in pluralism and its reliance on critical discernment in a joint effort to build a public world in pursuit of the common good. Hence, when I speak below of the public world, I am very much speaking of the world of citizenship, the world in which disciples of various traditions come together and hammer out in public discourse the shape of the common world they will all inhabit.

If a revised correlational practical theology is to bridge the gap between citizenship and discipleship, it should be at the same time *critical, public,* and *centered in theological ethics.* By *critical* I mean that, although practical theology must begin with faith and discipleship as formed by a community of believers, it must go beyond an unreflective attitude and seek arguable reasons for supporting its practical action. It must be *public* in the sense that it should attempt to relate the Christian message not only to the inner life of the church but to the public world in all its pluralistic, secular, and rapidly changing character. To do this, of course, it must all the more respond to the challenge of expressing itself in both the evocative language of faith and the critical language of public discourse. In saying this, I find myself both resonating with, yet distinguishing my position from, Walter Brueggemann's creative characterization in this volume of the language "behind the wall" and "at the wall." Brueggemann seems to equate these two languages to, respectively, sectarian language and the language of public discourse. But actually my distinction between the language of faith and public discourse is not exactly parallel to Brueggemann's language *behind* and *at* the wall.[4]

Brueggemann seems to believe that all language at the wall—all public language—is language under the control of a dominant and oppressive rationality.[5] I agree that much language at the wall or in public places is controlled by a dominant rationality that functions to exclude certain other languages. But such language, even though it occurs in public, is not genuine public discourse. The revised correlational method cherishes both the language behind the wall (the language of faith) and the language at the wall (the language of public discourse). It assumes that both languages are important and that each can be a source for testing the depth and universality of the other. Brueggemann seems to admit that the two languages can function this way when he tells us that Israel's Torah (the source of the language behind the wall) is an elaboration of "a common legal tradition in the Near East" (p. 16) which has now become the center for the life of the particular community called Israel. This seems to point toward a common moral language which can emerge in the public conversation at the wall and which has continuities or analogies with the language of faith. This is the possibility which animates the vision of a revised correlational approach to practical theology.

But finally, practical theology must *center itself in theological ethics*. It is my position that theological ethics is the center of the practical theological disciplines. It is the discipline that most self-consciously concerns itself with both the norms of human action and the norms of human fulfillment. Not only is it the case on logical grounds that theological ethics should be the center of practical theology but, in addition, theological ethics has made significant gains in our day and can be seen as the premier region of practical theology, because of its dialogue with, and use of, the powerful tools of moral philosophy.

Practical Theology and Theological Ethics

To elect theological ethics as the center of the practical theological enterprise requires amplification. First, the phrase "practical theology" was first used within the decision of the Lateran

Council of 1215 that each metropolitan church should appoint a *magister* who was to have the responsibility for penitential practice and the moral discipline of the church. This established a close relation between practical theology and moral theology.[6] This is a relation that lasted several centuries within the Catholic Church but fell upon hard times within Protestantism.

Second, to give theological ethics such a prominent place in practical theology is to state its centrality for all the other more specialized regions of practical theology such as worship, homiletics, religious education, and pastoral care. For instance, although there is a certain sense in which worship or liturgics is the most fundamental of the regions of practical theology as it is basic to the Christian life, it is uniquely dependent upon theological ethics for clarifying its implications for action. Worship can perform a variety of functions; it both legitimizes and renews our normative visions of everyday life. It provides a foundation to our view of how life should be lived. It renews that view and frequently helps to restructure it when our everyday world seems to break down. Hence, there is a strong structural component in any act of worship, as Victor Turner, Anthony Wallace, and Claude Lévi-Strauss have shown.[7] By "structural component" I refer to the wide range of both implicit and explicit understandings about how the social world both is and ought to be. Questions about the structure of the social world are basically ethical questions. Hence, to answer the question about the kind of social world that worship should confirm, revitalize, or create, it must resort to an implicit or explicit theological ethic.

Theological ethics is even more crucial for religious education (*catechetics*) and pastoral care (*poimenics*). Ethics involves two questions that are both of key importance for a proper orientation to those specific regions of practical theology. The discipline of ethics, whether secular or theological, must establish the principles, methods, and procedures necessary to undergird social praxis. In addition, the disciplines of ethics must help us answer the question of the nature of human fulfillment. According to standard distinctions made in moral theology, the first set of questions are "deontic" questions which try to answer the question of what we are obligated to do.[8] The second set of questions are "aretaic" questions which try to identify the nature of the good person and the nature of morally proper character, motivation, and virtue.[9] Since both religious education and pastoral care are types of social praxis, they are full of questions requiring objective (deontic) ethical decision making. Questions in pastoral care such as who should be cared for, how, when, and how often are basically moral questions. Such questions, sooner or later, need to be addressed by moral principles of a deontic type.

But even more important for both pastoral care and religious education are the aretaic ethical decisions about the nature of the good person and the nature of good character and virtue. If a central goal of Christian religious education is to help create Christian persons with virtues and motivations that will equip them for a certain kind of communal practice, then clearly a Christian ethics dealing with aretaic questions is fundamental. It is similarly fundamental to pastoral care. If pastoral care helps heal, guide, reconcile, and sustain broken or perplexed people, it must have various normative images of human fulfillment (the aretaic question) against which to measure brokenness and to understand health and wholeness.

The failure to anchor Christian religious education in the more fundamental discipline of practical theology and its key sub-discipline of theological ethics explains much of the confusion that has beset the educational task of the church. It has led us to fail to see Christian education within its proper disciplinary context. This has led us to overlook important questions about the relation of religious education to other regions of practical theology such as worship, care, homiletics, and social action. It has led us to see religious education primarily as an applied discipline. It has led many religious educators to believe they need not take responsibility for important but uncritical use of various social sciences. Not seeing itself as a practical theological enterprise, religious education has been somewhat blind to the fact that its central goal is to help form people into communities of practical moral thinking and action with a twofold interest in both discipleship and citizenship.

Religious Education as Practical Theology: Some Contemporary Statements

Practical Theology in John Westerhoff

Within the recent past there have been several efforts to state the nature of Christian religious education as an expression of practical theology. I will review some of these statements and evaluate them from the perspective of my initial remarks about a revised correlational approach to practical theology that gives a central place to theological ethics and that addresses the question of both discipleship and citizenship.

John H. Westerhoff, in his *Building God's People in a Materialistic Society*,[10] has presented a vigorous call to envision Christian education as a practical theological enterprise. "Education to be Christian," he tells us, "assumes an awareness of the process by which we make rational sense of ourselves and the world."[11] After making the standard distinction between fundamental, systematic, and practical theology, he divides practical theology into five dimensions—the liturgical, the moral, the spiritual, the pastoral, and the catechetical.[12] The usefulness of Westerhoff's proposal is found in his claim that each of these dimensions of practical theology is related to and includes all the others. For instance, it is possible to speak of the Christian education potential of each of the other dimensions of practical theology—the liturgical, the spiritual, the moral, and the pastoral. This is an extremely powerful idea and illustrates the usefulness of placing religious education within the context of the broader theological task.

I am especially interested in Westerhoff's understanding of the place of the moral dimension within practical theology as a whole and Christian education in particular. Following the work of the Christian ethicist Stanley Hauerwas and the Christian educator Craig Dykstra,[13] Westerhoff sees theological ethics as primarily an aretaic discipline. Hence, the practical theological discipline of Christian ethics has to do with understanding the implications of the Christian story for the kind of character that Christians are supposed to have. The moral dimension of the practical theological discipline of Christian education deals with forming the character of individuals by helping them appropriate, within the context of a Christian community, the full significance of the Christian story.[14] Christian ethics and religious education are, for Westerhoff, not primarily a matter of moral decision making, although of course they entail this eventually. They have the job first of comprehending and internalizing the characterological implications of the Christian story. Once this occurs, it is assumed that good decisions will more or less automatically follow.

In taking this position, Westerhoff is pointing to the importance of the practical theological discipline of Christian ethics for the practical theological task of Christian education but, at the same time, is taking a very particular, and I believe somewhat one-sided, approach to theological ethics. In his repudiation of all ethics of principle in the name of an ethics of character, it is not clear that he has given Christian education its full range of resources. For it is not certain that we must choose between principle and character in either theological ethics or Christian education. In fact, I will argue below that an adequate practical theology of either theological ethics or Christian education requires both. This is especially true if our practical theologies of education and ethics are to equip us for both discipleship and citizenship. Discipleship requires the Christian to be faithful but not necessarily articulate. But to be a citizen in a pluralistic world requires us to be both faithful and articulate about the grounds and principles of our actions. For this we need both an ethic of character and an ethic of principle.

Practical Theology in James Fowler

In an essay entitled "Practical Theology and the Shaping of Christian Lives," James Fowler also has placed Christian education within the context of practical theology and has taken a position strongly resembling Westerhoff's. Fowler defines practical theology as "critical and constructive reflection on the praxis of the Christian community's life and work in its various dimensions."[15] Although practical theology is understood by Fowler as critical reflection and in this sense seen as philosophical, it is both animated by and primarily addressed to the living reality of the faith community.

A practical theology of Christian education is seen by Fowler as critical reflection on the church's task in the *"formation and transformation of persons."*[16] It has its foundation in what the great metaphors of God the Creator, Governor, and Redeemer suggest for Christian character. In addition, it requires a theory of general faith development, a more specific theory of Christian faith development, and finally a theory of the methods and strategies guiding formation in faith. Fowler is similar to Westerhoff in emphasizing an interest in the formation of Christian character in contrast to more objective principles and methods constitutive of moral decision making. In addition to the formative influences of H. Richard Niebuhr,[17] Fowler too has been profoundly influenced by Hauerwas and, more recently, works by Bernard Häring and Don Saliers. In taking such a position, he is emphasizing the importance for Christian education of the aretaic approach to theological ethics.[18] Hence, although close to the position I will advocate, I will emphasize the importance to Christian education, as indicated above, of both deontic and aretaic approaches to theological ethics and moral theology. Further, in addition to affirming the importance of the confessing ecclesia as inspiring context for education for discipleship, I will emphasize a critical and public Christian education—one that will help Christians to be citizens as well as disciples.

Practical Theology in Thomas Groome

In his widely appreciated *Christian Religious Education*,[19] Thomas Groome has not set out to intentionally construct a practical theology of Christian education, but as a matter of fact this is precisely what he has done. The excellence of this book, in my opinion, comes from the seriousness of his effort in writing a theology of praxis that addresses the particular region of Christian education. It is also the case that in a recent essay he has more directly addressed the question of the relation of practical theology to education.[20]

Groome's practical theology of Christian religious education parallels to a considerable degree the details of my own approach briefly outlined at the beginning of this essay. He follows in a general way a revised correlational approach, and, in addition, his practical theology is critical, public, and centered in theological ethics. It is, however, Groome's tendency to overlook the full importance of the role of theological ethics in his practical theology that points to whatever difficulties exist in his outstanding work. For Groome, more than any other contemporary contributor to Christian education, has in effect anchored his educational theories in the practical theological region of theological ethics. But he has not adequately realized what he has done and therefore has not developed the fully worked-out ethical position that his perspective requires.

But before embarking on a discussion of this point, I will summarize briefly the ways Groome's practical theology of education can be understood as revised, correlational, critical, and public, and indeed aimed toward both discipleship and citizenship. First, Groome conceives of his educational method as entailing a dialectical conversation between, on the one hand, our own present praxis and personal story and, on the other hand, the implication for our praxis of the Story and Vision of the Christian faith. This should be seen as a hermeneutical conversation not unlike Gadamer's interpretative conversation between differing horizons of consciousness.[21] In one place Groome explicitly, although briefly, acknowledges the similarity of his position with the revised correlational method. He writes:

What I intend here is very close to what I understand Tracy to mean by "critical correlation." Tracy sees that there are namely, "the Christian fact" and common human experience and language. Both sources must be themselves critiqued and then critically correlated with each other.[22]

Second, as can be readily seen from the above quotation, Groome intends his practical theology of education to be critical. By critical, I take it, he means to affirm, yet go beyond, both a confessional stance in theology and a socialization stance in educational methodology. He is fully aware that faith first emerges out of the confessional stance of worshiping, believing, and practicing religious community—as Ellis Nelson suggests[23]—but he also believes that Christian maturity within the conflicting perspectives of a pluralistic society requires submitting our confessional beginning points to critical philosophical reflection. But Groome never speaks about the role of rational and philosophical reflection quite that explicitly. Instead, he does speak of such things as critiquing the Christian Story in the light of our personal story and critiquing our personal stories in the light of the Christian Story.[24] Such points suggest a critical, philosophical approach and do indeed raise the question of how it is actually controlled and made responsible. This consideration becomes somewhat acute when Groome admits that a practical result of this process of mutual criticism might involve going beyond in the Christian Story what he calls in one place its "lower echelon of the hierarchy of truths."[25]

And finally, Groome should be seen as doing a practical theology of Christian religious education that attempts to address the diverse publics of a pluralistic society. This can be seen, first, in his interest in a mutual critique between the Christian Story and common human experience. The result of this would be to present reasons for one's faith, especially for the practical and ethical implications of one's faith. But in addition, it means not only addressing the educational problems of the local congregation but being concerned as well from a Christian perspective about education wherever it occurs in our pluralistic and secular society.

But the ultimate success of Groome's attempt to be revised correlational, critical, and public depends more on an adequate theological ethic than he seems prepared to face. Groome fully acknowledges that his "shared praxis" approach to education is, as all praxis, a kind of political activity. But he does not provide an ethical methodology to guide this shared political and community forming activity. Groome's five movements in the shared praxis approach constitute a valid outline, in my judgment, for a practical theological methodology of a critical correlational kind. It is both a pedagogical procedure and a practical theological method. It makes teaching an exercise in faithful practical theological thinking and acting. Yet these five movements—(1) naming the group's present activity, (2) critically reflecting on its consequences, (3) presenting the Christian Story and Vision as it applies to the topic at hand, (4) dialectically relating this Story and Vision to the group's stories and visions, and finally (5) choosing a personal faith response for the future[26]—cannot become usable, especially on more complex praxis issues in the public world of citizenship, unless they are infused with a more discernible ethic.

Groome is partially aware of this and does present some guidelines on ethical decision making. They are suggestive but probably not sufficient. For instance, there are long and insightful discussions of the symbol of the kingdom of God and how both love and justice are seen to be dimensions of it.[27] But his discussions of love and justice are not fine-tuned enough. Groome seems to have little awareness of the large number of different definitions of both love and justice functioning in contemporary theological ethics. It would be difficult to analyze what he has said on either of these ethical principles in terms of some of the standard distinctions used in moral philosophy and widely employed in present-day religious ethics—distinctions that are important because they truly make a practical difference in how a principle actually functions.

Would more deontic approaches to ethics be the model Groome has in mind? This seems clearly to be the case in contrast to the more aretaic models functioning in Westerhoff and Fowler. Groome, in contrast to Westerhoff and Fowler, is not just interested in forming good people, although he is certainly interested in that. He is also interested in forming people who can think and act according to the objective requirements of the kingdom. But if his approach is more deontic, would rule or act deontology be more appropriate? Is act or rule utilitarianism closer to what he believes is required by the kingdom of God? Or is there some alternative model that he has in mind?

He does, at one point, give us three principles to guide the ethical dimensions of a shared praxis dialogue—"consequences, continuity, and community/church."[28] But what do these principles mean and how far do they carry us forward? By consequences he means to ask whether a particular praxis contributes to the coming of the kingdom. But this, it must be admitted, would be difficult to answer unless one had a more precise definition than given by Groome about just what kind of love and justice the kingdom entails. For instance, if justice were defined as the utilitarians and some situational ethicists (who are generally utilitarians) define it, then whatever action pro-

duces more overall good for the largest number of people would
be seen to have the best consequences.[29] But this definition of
justice would be seen by some deontologists, such as a John
Rawls or a Ronald Green,[30] as decisively unjust. So, without
more being said about the criteria for judging consequences, this
principle would not go far in enhancing decision making in a
shared praxis situation.[31]

By continuity Groome means that decisions "made by people
in a shared praxis group must be in continuity with the Story of
the Christian community before them."[32] But without more
discussion of the content of the central ethical principles of the
kingdom, one would lack the criteria to determine continuity. In
addition, there would be no critical way to determine whether
that which was continuous with the essence of the tradition was
also humanly and ethically justifiable. And finally, by com-
munity/church Groome means to suggest that decisions subject
to the guidance of the Holy Spirit both within the immediate
community and the larger ecumenical church will be sounder
than those made without this communally shared guidance.[33]
But we must ask, just how would Groome know that such
decisions are wiser unless they are consistent with some prior
understanding of the basic ethical principles implicit within the
kingdom? The point is that these three criteria cannot themselves guide praxis; rather, they assume principles and distinctions that Groome has not given us but that we sooner or later
would need. Hence, although there is a thrust in Groome's
important theory toward education for both discipleship and
citizenship, without a more specific theological ethic, shared
praxis in the complex public world of citizenship may be both
confused and inarticulate.

An Ethical Refinement of
Groome's Shared Praxis Approach

My high regard for Groome's practical theology of Christian
religious education stimulates me to try to refine his five movements with a more explicit theological ethic. To do this, I will
present a theory of the five dimensions of practical moral thinking, relate them to Groome's method, and then conclude with

some notes about the different pedagogical requirements that each of the five levels entails.

In a series of articles, and especially in *Religious Ethics and Pastoral Care,*[34] I have been gradually evolving a theory of practical moral rationality. Because I understand ethical thinking as always in some way assuming a larger worldview which it arrives at partially on faith, this theory also can be seen as the formal outlines of a practical theology.

My theory has both a deontic and an aretaic side. In this I agree somewhat more with Groome than I do with either Westerhoff or Fowler. It begins with the conviction that our aretaic images of good character are decisively influenced by prior images and principles about how the world really is and of what right moral thinking actually consists. This is why I begin with a presentation of the five dimensions of practical moral thinking stated in an objective mode and, after this is done, move to a more aretaic statement of the five dimensions. What follows must be compressed because of the limitation of space, but I hope it helps illustrate, with special reference to the work of Groome, the ways the practical theological region of theological ethics can help place Christian education on a more solid footing.

Over the last few years, I have developed the conviction that there are five dimensions to practical moral thinking:

1. A visional or metaphorical dimension
2. An obligational dimension
3. A tendency-need dimension
4. A contextual dimension
5. A rule-role dimension

These five dimensions constitute the "thickness" of moral experience. Moral experience is multidimensional. When we overlook this truth, we inevitably commit some kind of moral reductionism that distorts our moral discernment. In the thickness of actual experience, these five dimensions are woven into a seamless fabric. But they are distinguishable analytically and therefore susceptible to description.

These five dimensions are hierarchically organized in that the higher ones have more extensive influence over the total process of moral thinking than the lower. But, at the same time, each has a partial independence from all other dimensions, including the higher or more encompassing ones. By this I mean that, when critical moral thinking is actually taking place, fresh judgments are made at each of the five dimensions which are never simply logically derived from the higher ones. Nonetheless, each of the five dimensions is required for purposes of making actual, concrete moral decisions. The five dimensions complete one another and, at least to some degree, depend on one another.

The five dimensions arise from five fundamental questions that we implicitly or explicitly ask ourselves when we think freshly about praxis issues. The most fundamental question is, *What kind of world do we live in?* To answer that question, we must necessarily resort to metaphors and narratives that symbolically and dramatically represent the ultimate context of our experience. The second most basic question is, *What should we do?* To answer this, we resort to some general principle that tells us rather abstractly but comprehensively what we are morally justified in doing. We find such general principles in the Golden Rule and in the principles of neighbor love found in the second great commandment. We also find them in utilitarian and Kantian principles of obligation or in maxims of punitive reciprocity such as "An eye for an eye and a tooth for a tooth." The third question asks, *What are the basic tendencies, needs, and nonmoral values that human beings, because of their nature, seek to satisfy?* Such information is crucial for answering the question of which nonmoral goods and values are the important ones for our principles of obligation properly to mediate or adjudicate. Fourth, there is the question, *What is the present cultural, sociological, or ecological context, and what constraints does it place on our action?* And finally, after gaining answers to the four questions above, we ask, *What should be the concrete rules and roles that we should follow?*

In suggesting that these five questions are in some way present in all instances of relatively autonomous moral thinking, I do not mean that they are consciously so, nor do I mean that we always start with the higher or more basic questions and systematically go down from there. In fact, we probably generally back into the higher questions as we gradually move from the problem we are confronting to a more theoretical analysis of how we are *presently* thinking, and then how we *should in the future* think, about the issue that we are facing. In fact, we generally start out, as Groome suggests, with an analysis of our present action (what I call the rules and roles that govern our present praxis) and then move backward, in an effort to uncover our grounding assumptions, to a fuller analysis of the higher dimensions of moral thinking. This, of course, would be something analogous to the critical reflection on our Story and Vision that Groome refers to in his second movement.

My proposal is to differentiate what Groome has in mind by the Christian Story and our more personal stories in the light of these five dimensions. When this is done, the dialectical conversation that Groome envisions between the Christian Story and our individual stories can be more truly critical, and we can have a much clearer picture about what this conversation will truly consist of. For instance, to compare my story or that of my group to the Christian Story entails comparing my deep metaphors to the deep metaphors of the central Christian witness. It means critically correlating my actual principle of obligation to the principles of the Christian Story. It means comparing the tendencies and needs that I or my society value as fundamental to human existence with those deemed important by the Christian message. It would entail comparing contrasting perceptions of context and differing conclusions about rules and roles. It would be at these lower levels of practical moral thinking that we can expect, and rightfully, the greatest room for variation between our contemporary stories and the Christian Story.

But the possibility of critical reflection assumes that we can find a third perspective that constitutes a vantage point from which to test and evaluate both our own stories and the Christian Story. This reflective vantage point entails injecting a philosophical note into our Christian religious education. It is this philosophical note that is crucial to effect the transition from discipleship to citizenship, from faith to praxis in the public world. Let me share some of my own critical reflection about the Christian Story.

A Philosophical Perspective

The narrative line of the Christian Story is grounded in three basic metaphors that are used to represent the character of God's nature and action. H. Richard Niebuhr has suggested with good reason that the metaphors of Creator, Governor, and Redeemer applied to God are a useful summary of the deep metaphors of the Christian faith. These metaphors have communicated to Christians that they live in a world that is basically good, that God is morally serious, and that the world is open to change and is redeemable. As long as we stay at this level of discourse, we are at what I am calling the metaphorical or visional level of practical moral thinking.

But to say that God is Governor and morally serious does not say anything very definite for human behavior until we advance some kind of proposition defining the nature of that moral seriousness. When we do advance such a proposition or principle, we are dealing with the second dimension of moral thinking. This occurs when we advance a definition of justice or love that gives specificity to the Christian Story's metaphorical claims about moral seriousness. Here we find great variation between different theologians and different strands of the Christian tradition as to how to articulate the principles of obligation implicit within the Christian Story. It is my opinion that the most satisfactory answers to this question come from those who give some kind of Kantian interpretation to the Christian concepts of love and justice.

I find the theological application by Ronald Green in his *Religious Reason* (1978) of John Rawls's neo-Kantian principle of justice as fairness to be especially satisfying.[35] Justice as fairness is a deontological principle; it does not arrive at an understanding of either love or justice by asking which action will bring about the largest amount of nonmoral good, as do the teleologists.[36] Rather, it asks what is just or fair when the parties involved in a decision are impartial or blind to the particular benefits a decision might yield to them. Or, to say it differently, this principle tries to envision what would be fair no matter where one might stand in a particular social system. Green has argued persuasively that it is possible to articulate both the principle of neighbor love and the justice of the kingdom of God in the light of this understanding of impartiality.

Whether Green is correct is not an issue that I can settle within the confines of this essay. My goal instead is to illustrate a range of issues in the practical theological region of theological ethics for the practical theological region of religious education. To think critically about the dialectical relation between the principles of obligation of the Christian Story and the principles of obligation within my own story is to raise questions of just this kind. This is especially true if a practical theology of education is to take part in a public dialogue in a pluralistic society. The flexible relation between our visions and metaphors of ultimacy (the first dimension) and our principles of obligation (the second) can be seen in the fact that similar principles of obligation can be found within the context of considerably different metaphorical contexts. For instance, it is widely known that something like the principle of neighbor love and the Golden Rule can be found in different religious faiths attached to vastly different metaphors of ultimacy. Cooperation between diverse religious traditions can be achieved precisely because such flexibility exists between the five dimensions of practical moral thinking.

Love of Neighbor: The Relation of Visional and Obligational Dimensions

I can illustrate the relation between the visional and the obligational dimensions of practical moral thinking more completely by discussing further the meaning and function of the principle of neighbor love in Christian ethics. There is clearly an element of impartiality or equal regard in the command, "You shall love your neighbor as yourself" (Matthew 19:19; 22:39). This principle asks us to take the needs and claims of others with the same or equal seriousness that we take our own. The principle does permit us to take our own needs and wants seriously; the commandment seems simply to assume our right to love ourselves and to be concerned with our own needs and welfare. But it also tells us to give equal consideration to the needs and claims of others. So stated, the principle clearly has much in common with the neo-Kantian principle of justice as fairness—the principle that we discussed above. Further, although the principle of neighbor love is a hard and demanding ethic, it does not as such tell us how active we must be in searching out and meeting the needs of the other. Nor does it say we must sacrifice our own needs on behalf of the other. It does not, in fact, build a place for self-sacrificial love. It does not tell us to sacrifice ourselves on behalf of the other; it simply tells us to take the needs of others with equal regard to our own.

How, then, is the principle of self-sacrifice brought into the Christian life, an element that the symbol of the cross seems to demand? This is where, I believe, the metaphorical and visional dimension of the thickness of Christian moral rationality enters into the picture. The narrative of God's love as being so great that God took the initiative of reaching out to reconcile humankind with the Divine is represented in the story about the cross and resurrection of Christ. This story of God's sacrificial initiative expressed in the death of Jesus qualifies what neighbor love means within a Christian context. It means that we are not only to love our neighbor as ourselves but are to follow Jesus and actively work (even sacrificially work) to reconcile the neighbor and bring the neighbor back into a situation of equal regard and mutual love. The visional level of Christian moral rationality calls us to energize the mutual love of the love commandment with an active and self-sacrificial love. This sacrificial love, however, is designed to return the world to the original mutual love which the love commandment appears to require.

It is my position that the equal regard of neighbor love is the heart of a normative civil ethic guiding citizenship. It is also central to the ethics of the Christian life. It calls us to mutual love and equal regard for the other. Even though it is central to the Christian life, it is not unique to the Christian life. It is generally acknowledged that the principle of neighbor love was widely held as fundamental to the moral life throughout the ancient Semitic, Egyptian, and Greek cultural worlds. It is first stated in the Hebrew scriptures in Leviticus 19:18: "You shall not take vengeance or bear any grudge against the sons of your own people, but you shall love your neighbor as yourself." It exemplifies the fundamental nature of reason as applied to matters of morality. As Kant so persuasively argued, all ethical judgments presuppose this principle even though they seldom completely match it.

The ethic of discipleship is added to the principle of neighbor love by the narrative and visional structure of the Christian Story, especially the symbol of the cross. Discipleship entails taking the principle of neighbor love the second mile and even sacrificing one's good in an effort to restore the situation to the condition of equal regard and mutual love. Discipleship energizes citizenship; citizenship participates in both the mutual love of the Christian life and the structure of moral thinking available to the secular life. But without the self-sacrifice of discipleship, citizenship may fail actively to reach out to restore distorted situations to conditions of justice and equal regard.

With reference to the lower three dimensions of practical moral thinking, a few things need to be said to complete my illustrative remarks. If I am correct in arguing for a more deontological understanding of the Christian principles of obligation, one would still need some theory of the basic human tendencies and needs that must be fairly and impartially actualized (love) and mediated (justice). Further, one would need knowledge of one's social and ecological context, but not because this contextual knowledge can exhaustively determine or shape either our metaphors of ultimacy or our principles of obligation. The empirical disciplines which give us such knowledge should not dictate the content of the higher levels of practical moral thinking, but they can give us information about which of our conflicting tendencies and needs can be fairly actualized and justly adjudicated within the constraints of our present context.

And finally, when judgments at these higher four levels or dimensions are made, then we should have new critical perspectives from which to test and possibly transform the rules and roles of our present praxis. This is what a revised correlational approach to shared praxis in Christian education is really about. It is a complex process. We should enter into it with our eyes wide open. Even if the details of my own position on the content of these five dimensions are open to question, that should not obscure the validity of my main point: that a critical dialogue between our stories and the Christian Story would eventually necessitate a critical conversation on these five levels.

The Aretaic Perspective on the Five Dimensions

In spite of my concern to state the more principled side of practical moral reason, I believe there is a characterological counterpart of the five dimensions I have discussed. I am fully aware that to the Christian educator, the characterological analogues to the five levels is the subject matter of greater interest. It is precisely the task of Christian religious education, in contrast to religious or theological ethics, to form people who have the kind of character, inclinations, readiness, and knowledge necessary to approach the five dimensions of practical moral thinking from a Christian perspective. The formation and transformation of human beings into acting Christians is the task of Christian religious education. But what it means to be an acting Christian can be greatly clarified if Christian education is brought into conversation with the practical theological region of theological ethics.

I represent the correlation of the objective and aretaic perspectives on the five dimensions in Figure 1.

The Five Levels of Practical Moral Thinking
from a Christian Perspective

Objective	Aretaic
1. Visional or Metaphorical	1. Faith Development
2. Obligational	2. Moral Development
3. Tendency-Need	3. Emotional Development
4. Contextual	4. Perceptual or Ego Development
5. Rule-Role	5. Rule-Role Development

Figure 1

This figure suggests that not only can a characterological counterpart to each of the five dimensions of practical moral thinking be specified but that, in addition, each of these five aretaic dimensions has a developmental line. Not only is faith development the aretaic analogue to the visional or metaphorical level of practical moral reason but also faith, as Fowler has tried to argue, has a developmental line. Similarly, the obligational level of practical moral reason has a characterological counterpart in our capacity for moral reasoning; this too has a developmental line, as Lawrence Kohlberg, Carol Gilligan, and others have suggested. The tendency-need level of practical moral reasoning has a developmental counterpart in our emotional line of development as psychoanalysis in general, and especially the work of Erik Erikson, has shown. I believe that we can also trace developmental lines in our ego's capacity to perceive, interpret, and test the empirical realities of our environment and, finally, even a developmental line in our capacity to occupy and devise appropriate roles and establish appropriate rules. To suggest that there are identifiable developmental lines for these five levels of character is not to suggest that the lines are totally separate and distinct. But it is my point, following recent developments in psychoanalytic theory such as the work of John Gedo and Arnold Goldberg,[37] to argue that our development has different lines entailing slightly different psychobiological infrastructures which are themselves shaped and activated by different types of learning.

Types of Learning and the Five Levels of Character

It is a complex task to shape people who have the characterological readiness to participate critically in shared praxis guided by a Christian approach to the five dimensions. Of course, when it is artfully done, it does not seem complex. But when analyzed and reflected upon, we see clearly how complex it truly is to become not only a faithful disciple but a critically reflective citizen.

The learning entailed in faith development involves both socialization and structural change in our moral and cognitive thinking. If one were to look at faith development from the perspective of Stanley Hauerwas and John Westerhoff, learning as socialization would be the model employed.[38] Hauerwas's contribution has been to show how a community such as the church is the bearer of a vision which itself forms character for those who participate in that community. This character is the framework for how the individuals of that community discern the world. This discernment is their faith.[39]

Fowler adds a structuralist point of view to this process. Following Jean Piaget's structuralist theory of development, he demonstrates what the natural differentiation and complexification of our cognitive structures do to our faith development. He has shown that faith development is not just the result of socializing forces of a community; it also comes from the transformation of our intellectual operations as these operations function in the environment of our inherited communal relations and the kind of worldview that they imply. Fowler has shown that there must be sufficient freedom, pluralism, and diversity in our social experience for the cognitive tensions to occur which stimulate higher-level intellectual transformations.[40] But in making this valuable point, he sometimes overlooks saying strongly enough that unless our intellectual operations are working on significant visions mediated by trusted communities, this natural transformational process is not likely to occur or *at least* not occur in the direction he believes is normative. This neglect of the narrative and characterological aspects of faith development has, however, now been corrected by Fowler in his recent *Becoming Adult, Becoming Christian.*[41]

We should conclude, however, that there is no need to make a fundamental choice between the more dynamic and historical model of Hauerwas and the structuralism of Fowler to comprehend the nature of the formation of faith. The structuralist differentiation of our patterns of faith occurs within the broader interactions that socialize us into our communities of vision and character but sometimes transcend them.

Moral development also has both a dynamic and a structuralist dimension. There is little doubt that at its more rudimentary levels, moral development requires some of the dynamics of superego formation as Sigmund Freud first conceptualized this process. Attachments are formed and the internalization of the cherished values of loved ones occurs in an effort to ward off the threat of object loss.[42] But in addition, the differentiation and transformation of our intellectual operations working on the ordering of interpersonal conflicts must also be, as Kohlberg argues, an important part of acquiring more autonomous moral judgment. There is no need to make a choice between Freud and Kohlberg; they simply describe different phases of the moral development process. An understanding of both dimensions is needed for the purposes of Christian religious education.

Nor is there a need to make a choice between Kohlberg and the recent challenge to his position by Craig Dykstra.[43] It is my conviction that in virtually repudiating Kohlberg, and thereby repudiating the role of principles in Christian ethics, Dykstra has in effect collapsed my dimension 2 (principles of obligation and the development of our capacity to use them) into dimension 1 (metaphors of ultimacy, stories, and faith). My interest in distinguishing these two dimensions also functions to resist the idea that simple socialization into the Christian Story is itself sufficient to stimulate the differentiations and structural transformations necessary for our moral development in a pluralistic society. If we are to achieve either a critical discipleship or a critical citizenship, we must understand how our communities fashion and point our practical moral reason in the right direction (socialization), but we must also acknowledge how sometimes practical reason, stimulated by experience and the pain of both self and others, rises to heights of moral sensitivity that go beyond the insights of particular communities.

A discussion of the kind of learning involved in emotional development raises the question of the relation of emotional development and faith development. It is clear that both of them entail dynamics of affectional attachments, identification with meaningful relations, and the development of typical patterns and modalities for coping with desire and anxiety. Neither emotional development nor faith development can occur without the development of intense interpersonal relations which are, at the same time, afflicted with the common tensions, losses, constraints, and delays of gratification typical of all life processes. Both emotional development and faith development involve learning how to cope with these strains and threats to our object relations. The difference between faith development and emotional development is primarily one of perspective. When we speak of emotional development, we have in mind the psychobiological needs that we *bring* to the world; when we speak of faith development, we have in mind our developing picture of the world and its deep possibilities that our psychobiological needs *learn to expect*. Hence, emotional development is the subjective pole, and faith development the objective pole, of the self-world interaction or dialectic that marks the nature of experience. Fowler's contribution, once again, has been to show that we bring intellectual operations to this interaction and that these operations are at least a factor in the way our interpersonal relations witness to the deeper possibilities of the world.

Emotional development is crucial for the more objective process of practical moral thinking and action. Emotional maturity means in part having experiential access to one's own generic tendencies and needs. Although certain kinds of moral problems require that this experiential knowledge must be supplemented by more objective knowledge of human nature, it is still the case that there is no substitute for this experiential knowledge of our own needs. It is the presupposition of our empathy into the needs of others. It provides the empathic element in the command, "You shall love your neighbor as yourself." It protects our practical moral decision making from becoming too mechanical, rationalistic, and detached.

Yet, as I indicated above, intuitive knowledge of our own tendencies and needs does not necessarily lead to right moral action. It is only when this inner knowledge is guided and shaped by additional factors that healthy access to our own feelings and needs contributes to our moral sensitivity. Our own healthy emotional development needs to be enriched by empathic participation in the lives of others—in fact, in the pain and suffering of others. Further, (1) healthy access to our own feelings and needs (and, we should add, pains), and (2) empathic experience of the needs and pains of others, should be guided by (3) genuine moral principles of the kind we have discussed above. Healthy access to, and memory of, our own needs and pains does not automatically lead to a moral response to the other, although they are indeed a precondition for empathy with others. Unless we actually experience the needs and pains of the other, we can sometimes luxuriate in our own health and our own self-absorbed enjoyment and self-actualization.

As we will see in our analysis of The Church of the Covenant, which voted for sanctuary, and in Karen Lebacqz's analysis (in

both volumes) of the relation of pain to moral awareness, empathy and imaginative participation in the suffering and pain of
actual refugees had much to do with the decision to extend
hospitality to them.[44] This is the wisdom of all those current
theologies and educational methods which emphasize the importance of the role of experienced pain in the education for both
citizenship and discipleship. But empathically experienced pain
alone does not automatically engender a moral response. This
experienced pain can lead to retreat, horror, fear, overidentifica-
tion, mindless activism, and tampering, unless guided by genuine moral principles—principles that are themselves informed
by solid information and complex analysis of the situation of the
people we are trying to help.

At dimension 4, knowledge of a sociological, ecological, or
economic kind about our contexts is more properly informational than the kinds of knowledge required at the higher three
levels of character formation. The learning involved is more
directly cognitive. Although there is doubtless, in some way, a
role for instruction at each of the five aretaic dimensions, it is
most relevant at this level.

And finally, at the last level, we learn roles and concrete rules
most easily when we actually enact them. Every educational
process must have this more concrete level of participation when
we learn by doing. This is the great wisdom behind the renewal
of catechumenate models of education which Regis Duffy has so
effectively pointed to in his *Real Presence* and *A Roman Catholic
Theology of Pastoral Care*.[45] This is also the wisdom of doing
Christian religious education in the context of confronting actual
issues in moral practice, as was the case with The Church of the
Covenant discussed in *Tensions Between Citizenship and Discipleship: A Case Study.* Doing religious education in the context of
confronting real issues in practice actually forces the integration
of all the five dimensions of practical theological thinking, as we
will see in the use of the five dimensions to analyze The Church
of the Covenant. Most clearly of all, it forces us out of the clouds.
It brings us to make decisions about the concrete rules guiding
specific patterns of action.

But a revised correlational approach to a practical theology of
Christian education requires not only actual enactment of roles

and rules but critical reflection on them as well. To do this involves the learnings connected with a self-conscious practical moral theological method of the kind proposed in this essay. It entails referring back to the more objective appropriation of the five dimensions presented earlier in this essay. It is precisely my proposal that Christian religious education in the future be built on such a method and, at the same time, help teach such a method as a part of the intentional Christian living in a complex, modern, and pluralistic society.

NOTES

1. Daniel Day Williams, "Truth in a Theological Perspective," *Journal of Religion* 28 (October 1948): 241–54; idem, *The Minister and the Care of Souls* (New York: Harper & Brothers, 1961); and Seward Hiltner, *Preface to Pastoral Theology* (New York: Abingdon Press, 1958).

2. David Tracy, *Blessed Rage for Order: The New Pluralism in Theology* (New York: Seabury Press, 1975); and idem, *The Analogical Imagination: Christian Theology and the Culture of Pluralism* (New York: Crossroad, 1981).

3. Don Browning, *Religious Ethics and Pastoral Care* (Philadelphia: Fortress Press, 1983).

4. See, in this volume, Walter Brueggemann, "The Legitimacy of a Sectarian Hermeneutic: 2 Kings 18—19," pp. 3–5, 8.

5. Ibid., p. 13.

6. Wolfhart Pannenberg, *Theology and the Philosophy of Science* (Philadelphia: Westminster Press, 1976), p. 426.

7. Victor Turner, *The Ritual Process* (Chicago: Aldine Publishing Co., 1969); Anthony Wallace, *Religion: An Anthropological View* (New York: Random House, 1966); and Claude Lévi-Strauss, *Structural Anthropology* (New York: Basic Books, 1963).

8. William Frankena, *Ethics*, 2d ed. (Englewood Cliffs, N.J.: Prentice-Hall, 1973), p. 9.

9. Ibid.

10. John H. Westerhoff III, *Building God's People in a Materialistic Society* (New York: Winston-Seabury Press, 1983).

11. Ibid., p. 6.

12. Ibid., p. 9.

13. Stanley Hauerwas, *A Community of Character: Toward a Constructive Christian Social Ethic* (South Bend, Ind.: University of Notre Dame Press,

1981); and Craig Dykstra, *Vision and Character: A Christian Educator's Alternative to Kohlberg* (New York: Paulist Press, 1981).

14. Westerhoff, *Building God's People,* pp. 80–84, 93.

15. James Fowler, "Practical Theology and the Shaping of Christian Lives," in *Practical Theology: The Emerging Field in Theology, Church and World,* ed. Don Browning (New York: Harper & Row, 1983), p. 154.

16. Ibid., p. 155.

17. H. Richard Niebuhr, *The Responsible Self* (New York: Harper & Row, 1962).

18. See Fowler, "Practical Theology," p. 161.

19. Thomas H. Groome, *Christian Religious Education: Sharing Our Story and Vision* (New York: Harper & Row, 1980).

20. Thomas H. Groome, "Theology on Our Feet," in *Formation and Reflection: The Promise of Practical Theology,* ed. Lewis S. Mudge and James N. Poling (Philadelphia: Fortress Press, 1987), pp. 55–78.

21. Hans-Georg Gadamer, *Truth and Method* (New York: Seabury Press, 1975).

22. Groome, *Christian Religious Education,* p. 232.

23. C. Ellis Nelson, *Where Faith Begins* (Richmond: John Knox Press, 1971).

24. Groome, *Christian Religious Education,* p. 217.

25. Ibid., p. 199.

26. Ibid., pp. 207–31.

27. Ibid., pp. 35–51.

28. Ibid., p. 198.

29. Frankena, *Ethics,* pp. 14–16, 34–43.

30. John Rawls, *A Theory of Justice* (Cambridge, Mass.: Harvard University Press, 1971); and Ronald Green, *Religious Reason: The Rational and Moral Basis of Religious Belief* (New York: Oxford University Press, 1978).

31. For a succinct statement of the deontologist's argument against utilitarian theories of justice, see Frankena, *Ethics,* p. 41.

32. Groome, *Christian Religious Education,* p. 198.

33. Ibid., p. 199.

34. Browning, *Religious Ethics,* pp. 53–71.

35. Green, *Religious Reason,* pp. 131–32; and Browning, *Religious Ethics,* pp. 63–68.

36. Frankena, *Ethics,* p. 34.

37. John E. Gedo and Arnold Goldberg, *Models of the Mind: A Psychoanalytic Theory* (Chicago: University of Chicago Press, 1976).

38. For a foundational statement on the socialization view of Christian education, see Nelson, *Where Faith Begins.*

39. Hauerwas, *A Community of Character,* pp. 130–34.

162 DON S. BROWNING

40. James Fowler, *Stages of Faith: The Psychology of Human Development and the Quest for Meaning* (San Francisco: Harper & Row, 1981), pp. 151–211.

41. James Fowler, *Becoming Adult, Becoming Christian: Adult Development and Christian Faith* (San Francisco: Harper & Row, 1984), pp. 77–127.

42. Sigmund Freud, *New Introductory Lectures* (New York: W.W. Norton & Co., 1933), pp. 86–88.

43. Dykstra, *Vision and Character,* pp. 33–62.

44. See, in this volume, Karen Lebacqz, "Pain and Pedagogy: A Modest Proposal"; and idem, "Paul Revere and the Holiday Inn: A Case Study in Hospitality," in *Tensions Between Citizenship and Discipleship: A Case Study,* ed. Nelle G. Slater (New York: Pilgrim Press, 1989).

45. Regis Duffy, *Real Presence: Worship, Sacraments and Commitment* (San Francisco: Harper & Row, 1982); and idem, *A Roman Catholic Theology of Pastoral Care* (Philadelphia: Fortress Press, 1983).

6

Pain and Pedagogy: A Modest Proposal

Karen Lebacqz

I

To be a Christian is to be "inducted" into a "community of memory"—a community of disciples who share a common story.[1] From the essays in this volume, we learn that this discipleship includes the following dimensions. First, it involves the development of a special, "sectarian" language—a language "behind the wall" that can challenge dominant interpretations of reality.[2] Second, it involves certain basic affirmations regarding the role of the church, the centrality of Jesus as the Christ, the sovereignty and goodness of God, the place of prayer, and the reality of sin.[3] Third, it involves the attempt to nurture a certain character—the "assimilation and reappropriation" of the character, motivations, and dispositions of Jesus.[4] And fourth, it involves certain restrictions on behavior[5] and certain modes of reasoning or argument about behavior.[6] The net result of these dimensions of being a Christian is a "structural transformation" in who we are, what we do, and how we perceive reality.[7]

Such a structural transformation is the distinctive feature of learning, according to Brian Wren in *Education for Justice*.[8] Wren argues that learning is characterized not by the accumulation of information but by *changes in consciousness*. The goal of Christian education is changed consciousness working toward justice and peace. On this there is increasingly widespread agreement among educators. But if the goal is changed consciousness working toward justice and peace, what are the proper means to this end? What educational methods are consonant with the vision of being a Christian as presented in this volume?

For many years I have been both intrigued and troubled by the methods adopted by one teacher who wanted her class of young children to learn firsthand about the evils of racism and discrimination. This teacher did not lecture her young pupils on the horrors of racism. Nor did she tell moralizing tales and draw obvious ethical conclusions from them. Rather, she set up an experiment in the classroom.

On one day, all the children with blue eyes were subjected to discrimination. They were not called on when they raised their hands, their comments were either ignored or belittled, and they were purposefully omitted from some class privileges. On the following day, the same treatment was accorded to those in the class who had brown eyes. Thus each child had her or his turn at experiencing victimization and discrimination—at being ignored, overlooked, belittled, and rejected "for no reason."

It was a painful lesson for the children. I have long since forgotten all the details. But my memory suggests that some children were deeply wounded by this treatment: some cried, others felt unworthy and lost self-esteem, almost all experienced one form or another of pain.

What are we to make of an educational method that uses the deliberate infliction of injustice with full knowledge that such injustice will be a painful experience? Is such a pedagogical method consonant with Christian community and convictions as presented here?

Certainly, much contemporary educational theory would not appear to make room for such a pedagogical practice. The thesis that the *means* used in education must match the *ends* of education is becoming a widely accepted truism among Christian educators.[9] If education is *for* justice and peace, then only "just" and peaceful means are acceptable. Teachers are warned to watch for the "hidden agenda" transmitted by the atmosphere of the classroom or by the environment of the school.[10] Only a "democratically structured community" is considered a fit environment for authentic Christian education.[11] Roles of teacher and student are to be "unfrozen" through dialogue and mutuality.[12] The deliberate infliction of injustice, with full knowledge of its accompanying pain, seems to violate such cautions.

One education theorist sums up the growing consensus: "Justice demands that the method used to bring about such changes [in consciousness] must avoid the cultural oppression it is trying to overcome."[13] If discrimination is a form of cultural oppression that we are trying to overcome, then, on the consensus among educators, it would not be appropriate to use discrimination as a means of education.

I propose, however, that this teacher understood something very important to the process of structural transformation. Specifically, I propose that she understood something important in the education of oppressors. By "oppressors" I mean those beneficiaries of an unjust sociocultural system.[14] This teacher understood that certain experiences of injustice and pain may be the prerequisite to structural transformation for oppressors. Since I live and teach primarily in a context of oppressors, the lessons from this teacher are important lessons for me.

My own experience suggests that injustice and the pain that it evokes can be a very important learning tool. My experience also suggests that crucial structural transformations are often accompanied by pain. By pain I mean "acute mental or emotional distress or suffering."[15] Thus, from my own experience I would argue for the legitimacy of an approach to education that takes seriously both injustice and pain.

Further, I believe that there are theological grounds for accepting such a position. These grounds will be elaborated here by reference to a biblical text and by an appropriation of some liberation theology.

II

In my own experience, understanding the phenomenon of oppression has been an exercise in three acts. Each act involved a coming to terms with injustice. Two of the three involved experiences of pain around that injustice.

Oppression. The first act was coming to understand that oppression is a social reality. The setting for this act was a study of children with Down's syndrome. Reviewing the medical data on these children, I rapidly discovered that most of the data were drawn from institutionalized populations. Surrounding these children was an interlocking web of expert opinions in which inadequate data became the basis for further self-fulfilling prophecies.

The child with Down's syndrome was removed from the family and placed in an institution; lack of development was then attributed to Down's syndrome and used as "proof" of the poor potential of such children. Data and "expert" opinions built on each other until children with Down's syndrome were considered hopelessly retarded. Not for many years did it occur to anyone that the low mental age shown by these children might have been the result of conditions of institutionalization rather than the result of Down's syndrome per se.

Under such conditions, value-laden language multiplies: the birth of a child with Down's syndrome is a "tragedy," women "need" prenatal diagnosis so as to avoid the tragedy, the medical profession "battles" against such anomalies, and so on. A vicious circle develops—a circle of oppression.

I once shared the common assumption that children with Down's syndrome are hopelessly retarded. Unwittingly, I participated in the circle of oppression. As I undertook my study, however, I came to understand that Down's syndrome was not always as it was presented. I saw clearly that the qualities of low intelligence attributed to the disorder might as easily have been the results of life in an institution. I came to understand that children with Down's syndrome live in a circle of oppression. And so I came to understand that oppression is a social reality.

To understand this reality is to change perception. It is to undergo structural transformation. Never again will I see the world as I once did, for now I see it through the eyes of one who knows that oppression exists.

Oppressed. This study was my first approach to understanding the phenomenon of oppression. There was little pain in this experience, though there was certainly some outrage at what I discovered. But still I had little sense for my own role in the circle. Oppression was something "out there" in society, not something "in here" in my life. If I did not find myself to be an oppressor in the situation, neither did I draw upon any personal experience in order to identify with those who were unjustly treated. I was questioning the language of the dominant reality, but I was not yet recalling an "alternative memory" of oppression which could speak prophetically in this situation.[16] Though my righteous indignation was aroused, my sense of identification and hence my understanding of oppression as a phenomenon remained incomplete.

I share this story because I believe that this is where many well-intentioned North Americans are today. We have begun to use the language of oppression. We accept the fact that oppression characterizes our reality. But we do not yet perceive it as a *personal* reality. We do not take responsibility for it on a deep level, nor does it change the way we live, because it remains "out there" for us.

My hunch is that it will remain "out there" until we connect it to our pain. It is pain that often moves something from being "out there" to being "in here." Certainly this was so in my experience.

The second act in my understanding of oppression began when I joined an all-male theological faculty. My colleagues treated me with respect and made a conscious effort not to be sexist. Nonetheless, since I was neither fish nor fowl, rapidly my status became problematic: the "faculty" toilet (men's room) was clearly not for me; yet neither was the "staff" toilet (women's room). Was I to be exempted from pouring tea at school functions because none of my (male) colleagues would have been asked, or was I to be asked, as was traditional for women on the staff?

Such small incidents were the beginning of a new kind of appreciation of oppression. Over the years as the incidents multiplied, I began to recognize the personal pains of a very real form of injustice: sexism. I came to understand not only that oppression exists but that *I am oppressed*.

Just as children with Down's syndrome are labeled "retarded" and thereby belittled, so women are labeled "girls" and thereby belittled as though they were children. They are called "dear" or "honey" by total strangers who would never presume such familiarity with men. The mere fact of being a woman caused me time and time again to be passed over, ignored, taken for granted, judged unimportant, or treated rudely. I came to understand that my logical and rational skills would be doubted just because I was a woman. I came to understand that my lack of value would be brought home to me in a thousand ways every day until simply to say "I am a person; my perspective is valid" would be an act of courage, defiance, and liberation.

In short, unjust treatment—and its accompanying pain—led me to a crucial change of consciousness. The pain of victimization brought home to me a new consciousness about the phenomenon of oppression. Oppression is not just something that happens "out there" or that characterizes social reality. It is something that happens *to me* and that characterizes my reality. It is a structural phenomenon in society. But it is a structural phenomenon *in which I participate*. I am oppressed.

To understand this is to undergo a change in basic perception. It is to participate in that fundamental structural change which constitutes genuine education. Never again will I see the world as I once did, for now I see it through the eyes of one who knows not only that oppression exists but that she is herself oppressed.

Oppressor. But that is not the change that concerns me most here. Though I am oppressed as a woman in North America, my oppressions pale beside those of others.[17] I live and work in an oppressor society, and not everyone in that society will have the experience of being oppressed. The crucial question for education in North America is how we come to see ourselves as *oppressors*.

For me, this third act occurred because of a painful confrontation in which I was judged and found wanting. Having experienced myself as oppressed, I gave considerable attention to trying to teach others about the phenomenon of oppression. I tried to be sensitive to the needs of Asian and black students in my classes as well as to the women present. In particular, I tried always to notice and call on those students who seldom raised their hands in class, hoping to give voice to the voiceless.

Given an opportunity to preach at school chapel, I preached on oppression. I preached on the need for the voiceless to be heard. It was then that one of my students opened my eyes.[18] "Why don't you practice what you preach?" she yelled. "You preach about listening to the voiceless, but you don't listen to them in your own classes: you never call on me." Shocked, I started to defend myself by pointing out that she never raised her hand. And then the pain hit, the bottom dropped out, and I understood: the atmosphere in my classroom was so oppressive to her that she *could not* raise her hand. She had become "voiceless" in my own classroom. I was her oppressor.

Thus I came to understand oppression from yet another perspective: from a personal recognition and appreciation that *I am not only oppressed but also oppressor*. To understand this is to undergo a fundamental structural change. Never again will I see the world as I once did, for now I see it through the eyes of one who knows not only that oppression exists, and that she is oppressed, but also that she is herself an oppressor.

Pain, Injustice, and Oppression. The specifics of my experiences are not generalizable. Each person will come to her or his understanding of oppression through a different route. What is important is whether there is a common element in those experiences that yields changed structures of consciousness. In particular, is there something crucial to an appreciation and appropriation of oppression not as a general social reality but as a personal reality? How do we come to understand ourselves as *oppressed* and—most crucial—as *oppressors*?

My experience suggests that it is possible to gain appreciation of oppression as a social reality through ordinary mechanisms of education involving typical tools of research. Examination of data presented in academic studies using ordinary tools of logical analysis led me to question the dominant portrait of Down's syndrome and to pose a new understanding.

But the crucial step here is not the general understanding that oppression exists as a social reality. The crucial step here is coming to understand oneself as oppressor. Letty Russell says, "We need a pedagogy for oppressors designed to unveil injustice and social sin."[19] I would add that such a pedagogy not only must "unveil" injustice and social sin but must make those a *living* reality. The issue is not simply changed consciousness about oppression but metanoia—a change of heart in which oppression becomes a deeply felt personal reality. One can use the language of oppression without feeling it, much as the Assyrians could use the Hebrew language without being part of the community of shared memory and shared pain that gave meaning to that language.[20] The issue, however, is how one comes to "feel" oppression, to gain structural transformation on the deepest levels.

My experience suggests that this deeper understanding of oppression, one in which oppression becomes a lived personal reality, may require experiences of injustice and pain. The shock of recognition that one is *oppressed* and the shock of recognition that one is *oppressor* both are accompanied by pain. As Don Browning suggests, induction into the Christian story may not alone be sufficient for structural transformation.[21]

For example, most Christians are very familiar with the story of the good Samaritan. But as we hear this story read and discussed, we tend easily to identify with the Samaritan. We will be the "good" person who helps the needy one.[22] It is not until we hear the story and *identify with the priest and the Levite* that we will understand that we are oppressors. Thus, telling and hearing the Christian story alone is not enough for some crucial educational events.

III

Part of the reason that we do not identify with the priest and the Levite in the story of the good Samaritan is that it is painful to do so. We do not want to think that we are the ones who passed by. But such pain can be a learning tool. And I believe it is a learning tool for which there is support and precedent in Christian tradition.[23]

Latin American liberation theologian Enrique Dussel argues for the importance of painful confrontation:

I can read lovely Bible texts from the depths of my sinful totalization, and thus can, with my false approach, become more and more divinized. But someone suddenly charging into my world and telling me, "I have rights that are not yours" upsets me, disconcerts me, challenges me, demands that I go beyond my-self.[24]

Such a disconcerting experience, Dussel suggests, is a form of service. Indeed, it is the form of service that Jesus often prac-ticed.[25]

Disconcerting questions were precisely what my student of-fered me. Her angry words, "Why don't you practice what you preach?" are an echo of Matthew 23:3, in which Jesus accuses the Pharisees of hypocrisy: "They preach, but they do not practice." If we remember that the Pharisees were good, law-abiding, religious, dedicated people who were the equivalent in their day to contemporary North American churchgoers and church lead-ers, the parallel becomes even more evident. I am a "Pharisee"— a dedicated leader in religious education who at least makes an effort to be law-abiding and righteous. Jesus' words spoken to the Pharisees might be spoken to me.

In this passage from Matthew, the Pharisees are called "blind fools," "vipers," and "whitewashed tombs." These are hardly gentle or kindly words. They are angry words. At least in Matthew's account, Jesus used angry confrontation in much the same way as my student did and as Dussel urges. What is the point of this angry confrontation? Might it provide a pedagogical lesson for us?

We are not told that the Pharisees experienced pain as a result of the confrontation. Nor are we told that they experienced a metanoia as a result of it. Perhaps they did not. There is no guarantee that angry confrontation will evoke pain or that pain will cause metanoia. As Mary Boys suggests, Jesus' teaching evidences two primary characteristics: an "invitation to imag-inative participation" and a challenge that respects the freedom of the listener.[26] The listener is invited to imaginative participa-tion in which she or he might adopt new perspectives, but the freedom of the listener is also acknowledged. And this freedom means that not every listener will "hear." Metanoia will not always happen.

When, then, does it happen? What are the necessary ingre-dients for metanoia? When does the charge of "hypocrite" hit home and evoke changed consciousness?

I cannot answer this question fully. I am neither an educational theorist nor a psychologist. But my experience suggests that if metanoia did not result for the Pharisees, it did not result *precisely because* they did not experience pain when they were confronted by Jesus. Metanoia requires repentance, and repentance is painful.

However, this answer alone will not do, since clearly not every experience of pain evokes metanoia. Sadly, all too often painful experiences simply result in a "hardening of the heart" in which people retrench more deeply into their previous perceptions or positions. Our instinct when attacked is to defend ourselves. In defending, we draw back into previous ways of responding to crisis. We see only the danger in crisis and guard against it; we fail to accept the opportunity and open ourselves to it. This was a very real danger for me, since my natural instinct when attacked was to defend myself. Why, then, did my experience of pain in that confrontation evoke a change in consciousness?

Perhaps the answer lies in the fact that it was not just any pain but the pain of *self-recognition* that I experienced. Perhaps it is precisely because I have been oppressed myself that it was painful to recognize suddenly that I do to others exactly what has been done to me. "An important way of learning to think from the other side is to transfer one's own experience of victimization and alienation to that of the experience of others."[27] Our own painful experiences of being oppressed should surely make us more sensitive to the ways in which we participate in the oppression of others.

Consider, for example, the story of David and Bathsheba (2 Samuel 11:1—12:7). In this story, David covets Bathsheba. In order to possess her, he arranges to have her husband killed. It is the unhappy task of the prophet Nathan to confront David with his unjust use of power—his oppressive acts. Nathan does so by telling David a little parable about a rich man who slaughters the one ewe lamb owned and loved by a poor man. When David's anger is kindled toward the rich man, Nathan has only to say, "You are the man."

In an intriguing analysis of this story, David Daube argues that the oppression represented in Nathan's parable parallels the oppressions once practiced against David by the great king Saul.

Thus, the parable has precisely the impact of forcing David to recognize that he who was once oppressed has become oppressor.[28]

Some will hasten to point out that Nathan did not use angry confrontation in order to evoke David's recognition and repentance. This is true.[29] Part of the power of parables is that they can evoke imaginative participation in subtle ways. And this is why I do not argue that anger is necessary for the metanoia under discussion. My point is more modest: I simply wish to uphold the value of injustice and its accompanying pain as learning tools.

The pain that causes metanoia and recognition that I am oppressor is the pain of self-recognition. It is the recognition that I who am oppressed have become oppressor. It is the recognition that the very things I would least like done to me are the things that I do every day to others.

This is a kind of self-recognition that requires repentance. There is no way that one can "see" this reality without altering one's behavior. In biblical stories, altered behavior is often represented dramatically: David fasted and slept on the ground, Ahab tore his clothing and put on sackcloth. These are public manifestations of the pain of repentance—turning it from an inner experience into a public acknowledgment. These stories suggest that true metanoia cannot be a simple "change of heart" that has no public dimension. Repentance is not a private and internal act, it is a change in behavior.

The crucial metanoia for oppressors is that in which judgment is rendered,[30] is accepted, and causes a pain that requires repentance. The judgment has force precisely because the one judged knows that she or he was oppressed and has become oppressor. As one black South African puts it, Jesus will no longer be identified with us "when we have thrown off the shackles of oppression to become the new authoritarian controllers of the lives of others."[31]

Viewed from the perspective of an educational process, justice includes judgment as well as liberation: "The prophetic word of comfort for the oppressed is also a word of judgment for the oppressor."[32] "YHWH is the God who intervenes in history to destroy the unjust (*resa'im* . . .) and to save the oppressed."[33]

Christians in North America often do not like to hear that God judges as well as loves.[34] But biblical justice includes both aspects.[35] Education for justice must therefore attend to the word of judgment addressed to the oppressor and to the pain that may accompany that word. A pedagogy for oppressors must not shy away from experiences that permit recognition that we *are* oppressors. Such recognition may involve judgment, and it is likely to involve pain.

IV

But who is to bring words of judgment and evoke pain? Crucial to a pedagogy for the oppressor, argues Letty Russell, is "the identification of *significant persons* capable of stimulating growth in others by example, caring, and challenge."[36] Who are to be the "significant persons" who bring the challenge designed to evoke the recognition that one is oppressor?

In scripture, this is often the task of the prophet. It is, further, an unhappy task, usually accepted reluctantly. Whose task is it in the educational environment?

This is a particularly difficult question if we recognize that the challenge may have to cause pain in order to effect metanoia. We do not traditionally think it is the role of teacher to cause pain. Indeed, the idea is anathema to me and to most of my colleagues. Yet it is precisely what the teacher did when she set up the experiment on discrimination. It is one thing to argue for the legitimacy of injustice and pain as learning tools. It is another to argue that it is the role of the *teacher* to inflict injustice or pain.

Consider, for example, a teacher who invited a group of black singers to address an all-white class. Students in the class expected to hear a concert. Instead, what they got was an angry outburst directed at their racism. One young white woman burst into tears. "You hate me for no reason," she sobbed. "I've never done anything to you and yet you hate me."

Of course that was precisely the point: the white students were experiencing, in reverse, the unreasonable hatred that the white community perpetrates against the black. Here the teacher was not the confronter but merely provided a forum in which confrontation of oppressors by the oppressed could occur. The teacher was a catalyst or facilitator, but not a judge or a perpetrator of injustice.

In general, it seems to me that the agent of confrontation and judgment, and of its accompanying pain, should not be the teacher. Teachers in our culture tend to be professionals.[37] Professionals have power. I have argued elsewhere that the very fact of this power sets limits on what teachers may justly do.[38] In particular, I have argued that professional ethics can require a curtailing of the exercise of professional power in the interests of liberation.

This perspective suggests that it is not always appropriate for a teacher to confront a student, though it was very appropriate for my student, as the one with less power, to confront me. The one with less power can present the challenge that causes pain with more moral certainty than can the one with more power. As Brueggemann suggests, the sectarian Israelite community could speak a prophetic and painful challenge to the oppressor Assyria from its own history of pain. Israel confronts the empire from its own experience of oppression.[39]

This may explain why it was acceptable for Jesus, as "teacher" or rabbi, to confront, bring judgment, and cause pain. Jesus was not in a position of institutionalized authority over others. He could address them as one of the marginalized in society. Within a believing community of the marginalized, "behind the wall," an alternative reality can be nurtured which may imaginatively and critically interact with the dominant reality of the oppressor.[40]

But what about the teacher who did the racism experiment, then? This experiment involved the deliberate infliction of injustice and its accompanying pain. This teacher was indeed trying to "unveil injustice and social sin," as Russell suggests we should do when trying to educate oppressors. But the teacher's method for doing so involved the use of unjust treatment as a means. She was not simply a catalyst for confrontation of the oppressor by the oppressed. Rather, she attempted to use oppression within her own class to teach her students to "feel" oppression. Her experiment would seem to be a classic case of using unjust means.

Or was it? While each child had her or his turn at being the victim, all children were subjected to the same experience of victimization. If all were subjected to unjust treatment, at least the injustice was equally shared in the classroom. Thus, it was a "just distribution" of the experience of injustice. Perhaps, then, her technique is not as unjust as it seems at first. Justice was done in the long run, because the experience of being discriminated against and victimized was evenly distributed.

But what if the teacher had decided that the black students in the classroom already experienced enough oppression outside the class and she had therefore done the experiment only with the white students? Or what if she had decided that the girls experienced enough oppression outside the class and had done the experiment only with the boys? In such cases, she would not have distributed equally within the classroom the experience of victimization and its accompanying pain. Yet again we might judge that she was not overall unjust, since she was only trying to equalize the children's experiences of unjust treatment, discrimination, and oppression. While some experience oppression as a result of social reality, others will experience it as a result of the deliberate construction of a classroom setting. If justice means equal exposure to injustice and pain, then her efforts were "just" because they sought equal experiences for all the children.

So there are ways in which we can mitigate our judgment of the injustice perpetrated by this teacher. Note, however, that although experiences of injustice may have been "justly" distributed, they were nonetheless genuine experiences of injustice. The children knew that it was not "fair" for the blue-eyed ones to be ignored and belittled. The fact that the brown-eyed ones then had their turn at being the victim did not make the experience less unjust or less painful in their eyes. Deliberate discrimination against a portion of a class is an instance of injustice even when it will be carefully balanced on the following day.

Injustice is painful. Judgment can be painful. Both forms of pain can serve the cause of justice. When educators urge only "just" means in a classroom, it is important that they attend to the nuances of justice. I contend that some experience of injustice may be an important learning tool because the pain that it evokes can result in genuine appropriation of an understanding of oppression as a personal reality. It facilitates those deep structural transformations which are the distinctive feature of learning.

I do not urge that all teachers practice injustice in their classroom or inflict pain on their students. I urge only a modest proposal: that Christian educators take seriously the reality of injustice and pain and their possible usefulness as a pedagogical tool. An education for justice may not be as limited in pedagogical method as some educators assume.

NOTES

1. See, in this volume, John A. Coleman, "The Two Pedagogies: Discipleship and Citizenship," pp. 54–55.

2. See, in this volume, Walter Brueggemann, "The Legitimacy of a Sectarian Hermeneutic: 2 Kings 18–19."

3. See, in this volume, Bernard Cooke, "Basic Christian Understandings."

4. See, in this volume, Don Browning, "Religious Education as Growth in Practical Theological Reflection and Action," p. 139: "A central goal of Christian religious education is to help create Christian persons with virtues and motivations that will equip them for a certain kind of communal practice." Cf. Coleman, "The Two Pedagogies," p. 46.

5. Coleman locates these primarily in nonviolence. See Coleman, "The Two Pedagogies," p. 47.

6. Browning, "Religious Education as Growth," pp. 138–39.

7. See ibid., p. 155.

8. Brian Wren, *Education for Justice* (Maryknoll, N.Y.: Orbis Books, 1977), p. 7 (emphasis in original).

9. There is nothing new in the idea that means and ends must match. It is a familiar idea in the field of ethics, raising its head with great regularity in arguments about war and peace: if peace is the goal, then only nonviolent means can be used, for any other means would undermine the very goal sought. This is precisely the *form* of the argument now being used in Christian religious education to argue against any use of "unjust" means in education.

10. See, e.g., Margaret Gorman, "Moral Education, Peace, and Social

Justice" in *Education for Peace and Justice*, ed. Padraic O'Hare (San Francisco: Harper & Row, 1983), p. 168: "Educators for social justice may find their teaching undone if the students perceive that the moral environment of their school contradicts its teachings."

11. Russell A. Butkus, "Christian Education for Peace and Social Justice: Perspectives from the Thought of John Dewey and Paulo Freire," in O'Hare, *Education for Peace*, pp. 142–43.

12. Wren, *Education for Justice*, p. 27.

13. Ibid., p. 80.

14. In *Education for Justice*, Wren argues that the divide between the beneficiaries and the victims of our sociocultural system must be addressed in the language of "oppression" rather than that of "underprivilege" or "disadvantage." See also Gustavo Gutiérrez, *A Theology of Liberation: History, Politics, and Salvation* (Maryknoll, N.Y.: Orbis Books, 1973), pp. 81–88.

15. Definition 2b in *Webster's Ninth New Collegiate Dictionary* (Springfield, Mass: Merriam-Webster, 1983), p. 846.

16. Cf. Brueggemann, "The Legitimacy of a Sectarian Hermeneutic."

17. See Karen Lebacqz, *Justice in an Unjust World: Foundations for a Christian Theory of Justice* (Minneapolis: Augsburg Publishing House, 1987). See also Dorothee Soelle, *The Strength of the Weak: Toward a Christian Feminist Identity* (Philadelphia: Westminster Press, 1984), p. 99.

18. The student was a white woman who lived in and identified with the black community. For all intents and purposes, therefore, she confronted me as a black person.

19. Letty M. Russell, "Pedagogy for Oppressors," chap. 5 of her *Growth in Partnership* (Philadelphia: Westminster Press, 1981), p. 111.

20. Brueggemann, "The Legitimacy of a Sectarian Hermeneutic," p. 7: "His Hebrew was fake Hebrew."

21. Browning, "Religious Education as Growth," p. 144.

22. The Church of the Covenant found the parable of the good Samaritan a compelling parable. However, they interpreted it in terms of themselves as the Samaritan who would help bleeding and injured people. See Karen Lebacqz, "Paul Revere and the Holiday Inn: A Case Study in Hospitality," in *Tensions Between Citizenship and Discipleship: A Case Study*, ed. Nelle G. Slater (New York: Pilgrim Press, 1989).

23. There may be support in educational theory as well. "In order to challenge the culture of the oppressors in a more critical way," writes Letty Russell, "it is necessary to experience the results of that culture among those who must pay for it" (Russell, *Growth in Partnership*, p. 130). Russell does not explicitly mention pain here, but it is difficult to see how one could experience (not simply observe) the results of an oppressive culture among its victims without experiencing pain.

24. Enrique D. Dussel, *Ethics and the Theology of Liberation* (Maryknoll, N.Y.: Orbis Books, 1978; first published in Spanish in 1974), p. 21. By "sinful totalization," Dussel refers to the fact that we tend to think we are all that there is and therefore are divine. Such "totalizing" of our partial perspectives creates idols, which is sin (p. 17).

25. Dussel, *Ethics*, p. 21.

26. Mary C. Boys, "A Word About Teaching Justly," in O'Hare, *Education for Peace*, p. 100.

27. Russell, *Growth in Partnership*, p. 131.

28. David Daube, "Nathan's Parable," *Novum Testamentum* 24 (July 1982): 275–88, 284.

29. For a contrast, see the story of Elijah's confrontation with Ahab over Naboth's vineyard in 1 Kings 21. Here the angry confrontation is very direct: "I will bring evil on you" (1 Kings 21:21).

30. Note that judgment can be rendered either by oneself, as in David's case, or by another, as in the story of Ahab.

31. Mokgethi Motlhabi, "Black Theology and Authority," in *Black Theology: The South African Voice*, ed. Basil Moore (London: C. Hurst & Co., 1973), p. 126.

32. Russell, *Growth in Partnership*, p. 113.

33. José Porfirio Miranda, *Marx and the Bible: A Critique of the Philosophy of Oppression* (Maryknoll, N.Y.: Orbis Books, 1974), p. 96. Miranda has been criticized severely for emphasizing the judgmental aspect of God's justice. For example, J. P. M. Walsh (*Theological Studies* 36 [December 1975]: 825) suggests that Miranda should meditate on "vindication is mine."

34. For example, in her intriguing study of the parables of Jesus, Pheme Perkins argues that the "foolish" maidens of Matthew 25:1–13 were excluded from the celebration by their own acts but were not judged or condemned. This seems to me to ignore the specific statement: "I do not know you." See Pheme Perkins, *Hearing the Parables of Jesus* (New York: Paulist Press, 1981).

35. Indeed, Brueggemann would suggest that the word of judgment and the calculus of action-consequences is the common theological thread in the Old Testament, whereas the word of love and forgiveness is the minority voice. See "A Shape for Old Testament Theology, II: Embrace of Pain," *Catholic Biblical Quarterly* 47 (1985): 395–415.

36. Russell, *Growth in Partnership*, p. 134; emphasis in original.

37. Note that even in Christian education, we tend toward paid staff teachers, training, and technological equipment as signs of "good" education. Allen J. Moore argues that we exhibit a materialistic bias in many of our educational assumptions. See Allen J. Moore, "Liberation and the Future of Christian Education," in *Contemporary Approaches to*

Christian Education, ed. Jack L. Seymour and Donald E. Miller (Nashville: Abingdon Press, 1982), p. 118.

38. See Karen Lebacqz, *Professional Ethics: Power and Paradox* (Nashville: Abingdon Press, 1985).

39. Brueggemann, "The Legitimacy of a Sectarian Hermeneutic," pp. 14–15.

40. Ibid.

Postscript

7

A *"Concluding Unscientific Postscript"*

Sara P. Little

W<small>HAT</small> S<small>ØREN</small> K<small>IERKEGAARD</small> did in his monumental *Concluding Unscientific Postscript to the Philosophical Fragments* was far more than a postscript to that small evocative volume in which he raised the question, "How far does the truth admit of being learned?" What he did in *Fragments* was to engage in a "project of thought" involving the reader in an ever-deeper reflection on how and whether one can indeed be brought into a relationship with truth. In the *Postscript,* he pursued that concern around an investigation of "how to become a Christian," taking a substantive next step elaborating on his ideas. There is a sense in which this present volume, *Education for Citizenship and Discipleship,* shares with its companion volume, *Tensions Between Citizenship and Discipleship: A Case Study,* a deep, underlying concern about truth and faithfulness and the role of education in relationship to the "becoming" of the Christian—although not in the categories posed by Kierkegaard.

This volume, *Education for Citizenship and Discipleship,* deals with other basic questions as well. But there is no sense in which this chapter is an elaboration on or a building of new theses about what has already been presented.[1] Nor is it a summary or evaluation. It is, instead, a more ordinary postscript. It is an effort to seek themes and concerns that may serve as a kind of springboard for continued and expanded discussion of subject areas opened up in the book. It is an invitation to join in the "thought experiment" of the authors, to participate in a dialogue in which the service of the mind is offered to the glory of God.

The dialogue as experienced by members of the National Faculty Seminar has not been a painless affair, a matter of stimulating and impressive conversations carried on as representatives of the Academy. In the move from the organizing question (introduced by Mary Boys in her editorial preface) to two volumes of essays, participants ran the risk of offering cherished ideas, of exploring new concepts and language of partner disciplines, and of experiencing vulnerability, but most of all, of *caring* about the church and the major agenda items for educational ministry of these last decades of the twentieth century.

The initial question, "How might our activities of interpreting the Christian faith educate for the future good of the world?" finally focused on "discipleship and citizenship," in its "organic unfolding process." In that process, at least two things became apparent:

1. In the final analysis, education requires the move from the general to the particular, from the vision to concrete enactment and testing. Thus the case study of the sanctuary event in The Church of the Covenant, recorded in *Tensions Between Citizenship and Discipleship: A Case Study*, became one of the most important aspects of the life and work of the National Faculty Seminar, perhaps the most important. To the degree that the particular case feeds back into and helps one understand or reformulate the generalization, knowledge is constructed. Moreover, education has "happened" when there has been reflection on the "particular." Thus readers should note that essays in this volume interact with, and benefit from, the reports and analyses presented in *Tensions Between Citizenship and Discipleship.*

2. Education itself is a mediating activity, or a field that calls for synthesis, as Mary Boys points out in "Religious Education: A Map of the Field."[2] It is hard now to imagine an equally effective way of reflecting on or shaping church education for the future than was found in the interaction of persons speaking from the

perspective of varied disciplines. Although the assumption that such would be the case lay behind the setting up of the Seminar, it has been confirmed in the experience of the group and points a direction for the future.

What I propose to offer in this concluding chapter are some reflections on recurring themes, all developed more fully in the individual essays, pointing both to the interdependence of the essays and to the ultimate integrative nature of the question itself. Look again at the starting point for the Seminar: "How might our activities of interpreting the Christian faith educate for the future good of the world?" That global question is used here as a frame of reference, with frequent connections to "discipleship and citizenship," because it was the context out of which the focus emerged and because it evoked explorations not included in the final report. For example, early interest in hermeneutics raised questions about the impact of media on perception and the resulting "interpretative filter." That was not the direction taken, as may be observed in the report that follows, and it is important to note that many other basic issues are yet to be dealt with in the generating question. Another example: Questions periodically appeared about developmental theory and its appropriateness for use in Christian education, along with the role of social sciences generally. They were never the subject of major investigation but were dealt with from time to time in other contexts.[3] The broader perspective allows for references to the Seminar and its activities as a whole.

I might summarize my postscript by identifying the following five topics:

1. Hermeneutics: Education as Interpretation
2. To What End: The Goal of Education
3. Conceptual Structures: Discipleship and Citizenship
4. Pedagogy: The Educational Process
5. A Question: Why Congregational Education?

Let me fill in the contours briefly by expressing this in one paragraph. The focus on hermeneutics indicates that the tradition we receive is an inherited interpretation, available to others as they reinterpret and thereby assimilate and reform the heritage. What persons intend to do with that heritage, the purposes for which they seek education and seek to educate others, is of critical importance. Clear conceptual structures delineate emphases and help give focus to the activities to be undertaken during any given historical period. Understanding why certain activities are appropriate and others inadequate is essential to the educating process. Finally, the need for a promising focus for educative activities leads to the congregation, with its potential for being a center related to a kind of network of intersections where people learn and ministry occurs.

1. Hermeneutics: Education as Interpretation

Whatever else can be said about Christian education, it seems clear that it has to do with "interpreting the Christian faith." That is to say, it has to do with hermeneutics. Assumptions or questions about the purposes and processes of interpretation never ceased to appear throughout the life of the National Faculty Seminar. What part does the corpus of the Christian faith play in interpretation? How does the dynamic inner reality called "faith" come to be? Why and how does "faith seek understanding"? How is that seeking, that understanding, influenced by the context, experience, memory, and embodied values in the community? Or to say it another way, what are the formative influences and the boundaries within which interpretation occurs?

"Hermeneutics" is currently a much-used category in the work of several fields or disciplines, not just in Christian education. How does Christian education carry out its "activities of interpreting the Christian faith"? The way that question is answered is in part dependent on one's understanding of Christian education. Mary Boys's essay, offering both a historical perspective and a contemporary "mapping," gives an important set of categories for analyzing approaches to education. The "classic expressions" she delineates offer alternative avenues to interpretative activities.[4] Obviously, the assumption is that there is no single way to "do" education. From time to time, people move to the conviction that certain methodologies are the favored or highly recommended approaches needed at a given time. For example, Don Browning, in his essay, makes that assumption in his elaboration of a plan for "practical theological reflection and action," a plan with quite definite hermeneutical implications.[5] The view of education implicit in Bernard Cooke's essay, "Basic Christian Understandings," has a major component that impinges upon hermeneutics. His basic presupposition for his essay, he says, is that "people need relatively few basic religious understandings; but *these few must be true.*"[6] Sociologists James Borhek and Richard Curtis would agree that belief becomes dysfunctional unless it is held to be true and is confirmed in experience.[7] For Cooke, the lifelong process of relating knowledge and experience is a hermeneutical activity that cannot and will not be sustained unless there is a conviction, continually reaffirmed, that what one understands is indeed true. That may be said to be a basic presupposition of all interpretative activities related to Christian education. And another such basic presupposition voiced by Boys, in her explication of her own position, is that *imposed* interpretation is not interpretation at all.[8]

Don Browning, in an even more direct way than Mary Boys, proposes that Christian religious education is inextricably related to questions of interpretation. His "revised correlational method" seeks to relate the "interpretation of the central Christian witness" with the "various interpretations of ordinary human experience."[9] It is precisely in the correlation of these two realms that Browning sees Christian education as practical theological reflection, not practical in the sense of "applied systematics" but practical as a specific methodology involving theological reflection that is centered in or (as he seems to prefer) "in conversation with" theological ethics. Christian religious education, according to Browning, has as its task the "formation and transformation of human beings into acting Christians."[10] His proposed methodology is a contribution to that task, through its complex process of interpretation. It is particularly instructive in the hints Browning gives as to ways of relating discipleship and citizenship.

Before the terms "discipleship and citizenship" even appeared in Seminar conversations, Walter Brueggemann raised a critical hermeneutical question. A particular sectarian community, one with its traditions and memory, inevitably interprets life out of its own perspective. In what sense is that sectarian hermeneutic legitimate? The Seminar asked for his position on that question. Brueggemann's imaginative answer, based on an exegesis of 2 Kings 18–19, provided terms that quickly became a part of the common language shaping the Seminar's understandings and commitments. The language "behind the wall" was the sectarian language constituting the Hebrew community, making possible worship, repentance, grief, prayer, and a seeking to be faithful to God. The public language of negotiation "at the wall" called for ability to communicate with those who spoke another language from other bases. The believing community had no special advantage in dealing with the public, and should not have.

The new set of categories opened doors for insights as minds made great leaps to the present situation. Public discourse (the conversation "at the wall") is not to be confused with the exploration of issues of faithfulness (the conversation "behind the wall"). Each conversation is legitimate, has its own language, and is in need of critique. Brueggemann's analysis of the two conversations and their relationship is too intricate and too essential in its details to be pursued here. What must be said is that his analysis leads to a call for church education of the future to be bilingual. It is to offer help both with the conversation "behind the wall" (the "language of transformative imagination") and with the conversation "at the wall" (the "language of policy formation").[11] The sectarian hermeneutic is basic, employing primal language, and has the power to move persons into the public arena made free from "perceived vested interests." It is not difficult to see how terms of "discipleship" and "citizenship" began to appear, and eventually to be explored directly.

Hermeneutical concerns were vividly focused when members of The Church of the Covenant met with the Seminar to discuss their decision to grant sanctuary (see the companion volume, *Tensions Between Citizenship and Discipleship: A Case Study*). They tried not to consider public policy in their conversation "behind the wall," a conversation nonetheless opened to the public. How did their understanding of the Christian tradition influence that decision? How did their action cause them to reinterpret, and perhaps appropriate anew, that tradition? Was there a flawed or an accurate interpretation of biblical texts which influenced the form of the action?

Those questions were considered in reflecting on the "sanctuary event," feeding into the conclusion that an individual's own personal stance functioned as a powerful filter through which responsibilities were interpreted and understandings developed. The hermeneutical process, whatever its beginning point, can never function productively aside from attention to the individual's perspective.[12] Again, there must be moments of consolidation of what is learned. Church of the Covenant members said their presentation to the Seminar was, for them, "evaluation"—a time when they reflected on their experience and sought to understand it.[13] Such times offer a sense of achievement, of establishing a "post" from which the next travel path may emerge, and a motivation for undertaking the travel. When something comes to be "understood," there is power to continue the process of interpreting and acting on the Christian faith. Hermeneutics and education are mutually enriching concepts and activities.

2. To What End: The Goal of Education

The original Seminar question explicitly stated the assumption that education is to be "for the future good of the world." Among other assumptions, some arising out of the interrelationship of hermeneutical concerns and questions of purpose, this affirmation of care for the world helped move the discussion into some of its most productive moments. Indeed, what is Christian education *for?* Historically, in all societies and all education, there is to be found a "conserving" aim, emphasizing the initiation into and preservation of a tradition, and a "transforming" aim, emphasizing human development and/or reformation of society. More accurately, some combination of these two emphases, some location on a continuum between the two, is the way to begin analysis of purposes. For Christian education, that question of purpose is a perennial concern. George Albert Coe focused the issue precisely in his question: "Should the primary purpose of Christian education be to hand on a religion, or to create a new world?"[14]

Perhaps without conscious intention, the framers of the "generating question" were expressing a concern about what is increasingly recognized as a kind of domestication of church education. The kind of care for the public good, long evidenced in educational enterprises of the church, all the way from support of public education to the effort to educate leadership for the nation, somehow seems quietly to have moved toward maintenance of an institution and—as nineteenth-century pastor-theologian Horace Bushnell would have said—to taking over the functions of the home.[15] In any case, the effort to be deliberate about the "future good of the world" was decisive for the direction taken by the Seminar.

A consensus about commitment to the "future good of the world" expressed itself in varying formulations and raised cautions and guidelines. Mary Boys's reference to the *"intrinsic linkage between traditions and transformation"*[16] picks up a theme that is common to all the writers, some more explicit than others. In no case is there a direct causal relationship between the two. The complexities are cited most clearly by John Coleman in his chapter on discipleship and citizenship. Karen Lebacqz speaks of "changed consciousness working toward justice and peace" as finding increasing acceptance among educators as "the goal of Christian education."[17] That would surely be a goal, if not the only goal, of Seminar members. It is also true that many church members today would be disturbed to think that education had to do with anything other than "shoring up the status quo," seen by Mary Boys as the polar opposite of the view that "traditions are for the sake of changing the religious community and world."[18]

To approach the matter from a somewhat different angle: What is the source from which we are to seek clarity about what is meant by "the future good of the world"? What difference does it make whether education functions more to hand on a tradition or to transform persons and society? If discipleship and citizenship are indeed focal points for education, how are we to determine what it is that we as Christians are to offer "the world"? Those who read (and reread) Bernard Cooke's "Basic Christian Understandings" in struggling with those questions will begin to see at least a tentative answer to those questions:

we seek answers in the gospel. What that means, then, educationally, is that we must seek to *understand* the gospel. Or if we ask the question about the purpose of education, we are led, as Cooke says, to the conclusion that "what is common to all situations of religious instruction is the goal of *understanding* what religion, specifically Christianity, is all about."[19] Cooke is talking about that "personal understanding of the reality of God acting in human life" that involves both knowledge *about* God and knowing God.[20] Such understanding comes through the experience of being disciples of Christ and members of the body of Christ. What Cooke does is certainly not to propose tests of orthodoxy. Rather, in his five basic understandings, he is making available his theological scholarship in terms that will help people "deal religiously with the experienced reality of their human life."[21] Disciples, just by being disciples of Jesus Christ, followers of the Way, care for the world.

3. Conceptual Structures: Discipleship and Citizenship

When the terms "discipleship" and "citizenship" emerged in National Faculty Seminar discussion as focal points for Christian education in the future, there was an affirmative response to the "rightness" of the categories for this moment in history. They became the organizing centers for concepts that provided tools for thinking. Because "education" is such an elusive term, prone to move in many directions, there is great need for conceptual structures that provide focus, limits, and the possibilities of cognitive clarity. In any case, the categories served that purpose for the Seminar. There was and is no attempt to be comprehensive, to rethink the totality of the enterprise called Christian education. Rather, the more modest effort of pointing to emphases appropriate for helping to deal with critical issues today is the intention.

What John Coleman sets forth in his explication of discipleship and citizenship and their interrelationship is extraordinarily evocative. The rethinking of what is meant by those terms logically calls for certain educational activities, which Coleman calls the "pedagogy of discipleship" and the "pedagogy of citizenship." Translating his comments into the realm of church education, one might say, for example, that discipleship presupposes devotion to the Teacher of whom one is a disciple. And the nature of that Teacher (in this case the Triune God) is of the utmost importance. Faithfulness is the mark of the disciple. The teachings are guides to meaning and forms of that faithfulness. The community of disciples is the location where believers struggle to interpret the teachings, to worship, and to nurture one another in faithfulness, including obedience. Although the parallels are not exact, it is possible to see some connections with the conversation "behind the wall" and the activities that characterize the life of the believing community. Failure to develop the "primal language" of that community and the "basic understandings" that constitute its memory and hope is likely also to be a failure in "doing the truth." Thus education for discipleship is basic.

Education for citizenship, particularly the "pedagogy of citizenship" as carried out by the church, also calls for clear delineation of what is meant by key concepts. Achievement of such clarity is surely the first step in planning for education. Every essay in this volume contributes in some way to such a task, although Coleman offers the most direct consideration of terms. What do we mean when we talk about the Christian citizen? More than likely, a Christian who is also a citizen. Then who is a citizen? Coleman goes beyond a view of citizenship as membership in a particular society, thereby involving the rights and responsibilities of that membership, to include what he calls "neighbor love," the "key to any correlation between discipleship and citizenship."[22] Like Brueggemann, Coleman calls for "bilingual education for the future." Such an education would make possible both the conversation "behind the wall" and that "at the wall." But Coleman's "citizenship" is not to be equated with the conversation of Judah and the Assyrians "at the wall."[23] For him, discipleship and citizenship are two "zones," which are "semiautonomous yet interrelated." The task of seeking to understand these two concepts or two zones is in part to become engaged in the educative process itself; and to use such resources and strategies as those illustrations from *Vamos Caminando*[24] is to test out the ideas and build back into greater clarity. To develop pedagogies for both discipleship and citizenship, in relationship to each other, is, according to Coleman and members of the Seminar, to "educate future generations to work for the betterment of the world."[25]

4. Pedagogy: The Education Process

How is pedagogy to be understood and developed? For Thomas Green, Seminar member, pedagogy is "simply the reasons for doing what we do in teaching . . . the explanation of a practice."[26] Green's intention was to write an essay dealing with the pedagogies of congregational education, including the pedagogies of discipleship and citizenship. The essay took on a life of its own and is on the way to becoming a book. It will carry on the conversation and, as now anticipated, will bring into being another set of conceptual structures to be employed in thinking about and planning for education. In his working papers presented to the Seminar, Green sees *norm*, *text*, and *liturgy* as three elements characterizing congregational education. The explanation of those terms will point to "distinctive pedagogies" and possibly to corresponding epistemologies.

Although Green's completed work is not available, it is apparent that other Seminar members dealt with pedagogical questions. Certainly in discussion, references to pedagogy were frequent. How are we to overcome the fragmentation that brings confusion in understanding and dissipation of energy in much of life today? Should not the community of disciples be a spot where one finds wholeness and direction in perspective? This spot, as Brueggemann says, is the "community of commitment," where one can do "grief work," can pray, can hear the prophetic word and use the "communal language" of memory and of hope. Such a context is the basic presupposition of any approach to pedagogy.

Actually, most of the essays deal in some way with pedagogy. There are clues as to attitudes, boundaries, expectations, and methods. For Mary Boys, pedagogy could never be viewed as eliciting certain predetermined responses from people. Her attitude is that of respect for tradition and for individuals. She calls for the use of "disciplined imagination" in making it possible for people to understand, to decide, and to make connections between tradition and transformation.[27] Teaching is an art, springing from the wonder of the teacher in the presence of transcendent mystery which can never be penetrated but can undergird and transform the believing community.

Imagination plays an equally important role in the work of Walter Brueggemann. To speak of hermeneutics, for him, is to call for imagination, essential for dealing with "depth of ambiguity and relativity in every process of reading reality."[28] However, one needs to *study* Brueggemann's use of imagination in his essay rather than to inquire what he says about imagination.

There are limits as to what can be accomplished through education, a process actually dependent on so many other factors that there was certainly no expectation in the Seminar that education in and by the church could take on a kind of messianic halo. But certain things *can* be accomplished through appropriate pedagogy, developed to help people *understand*, in the sense of the broad interpretation and the levels of activities suggested by Cooke. The effort to achieve clarity throughout the Seminar would suggest endorsement of Cooke's position. His concluding sentences are an important contribution to questions both of purpose and of pedagogy: "Understanding of itself will not suffice. Knowledge is not a virtue, but authentic Christian faith and life exist correlative to an accurate understanding of the gospel."[29]

Much of Don Browning's analysis of the five dimensions of practical moral thinking has direct links to pedagogy. Although he is directing his efforts toward reconceptualizing the field of religious education, and thereby rooting it firmly in the theological disciplines, some theological professors are already experimenting with using his categories as analytical tools and sources for questions guiding theological reflection.[30] Certainly his position centering such reflection around theological ethics could be a way of dealing with both discipleship and citizenship. And there are other indirect implications for pedagogy in his essay.

Karen Lebacqz deals even more directly with the matter focusing on the role of pain in pedagogy. Why not insight, joy (in the deep sense that comes from understanding), subjectivity as the truth for *me*, connectedness, awareness, empowerment for obedience, or a host of other possibilities? Precisely because pain is a neglected aspect of education. And pain is so characteristic of the history that constitutes the Jewish and Christian communities, not only in their experience but also in their interpretations, that it is ignored at our peril. Lebacqz's "modest proposal" is both a corrective to education and a direction. Agreement about the need for such an essay may be in part a reaction to the superficial and sentimental interpretation of the Christian faith often presented in the media, part of popular culture that seems far removed from either discipleship or citizenship.

Her essay calls forth a reflective response, with critical questions for all who dare to be called teacher. As teacher, when I look at my own motivation and performance, I can only confess my limitations—indeed, my sinfulness—and find courage to try again. But far more important, when I "see" and interpret faithfully, I am myself judged by the Truth—I and those whom I seek to teach. The pain comes from our confrontation by Truth. Like the Tanzanian woman described by Hans-Ruedi Weber as saying that the Bible is the only book "which reads me,"[31] we who are called to teach are "read" by that which we teach and learn.

Perhaps there are other unexplored areas that we need to consider as we look to the future. We know that the disciplined effort to understand always involves "painful thought." There is both pain and joy—sometimes the two are indistinguishable—in the "passionate conviction" underlying understanding, which unites the depth of reason with the affection of commitment. Will that still be the case with the creatures into which we are being reshaped by media? Computers raise the question about what it means to be human. Indeed, there *are* other areas to be explored in the conversations that we hope follow the publication of this book.

5. A Question: Why Congregational Education?

Throughout all the discussions of the Seminar, the idea that congregations are crucial for education seemed to gain momentum. In particular, the focus on discipleship and citizenship pointed toward congregations. Why do we use the term "congregation" instead of church education or Christian education or catechetics or catechesis? Those terms have been used throughout history to point to at least some of the same activities that we speak of in connection with congregational education. It may be that the general popularity of the term, evidenced in discussions as well as in numerous writings,[32] has influenced Seminar members. More likely, however, it is the case that activities in which the Christian faith is experienced, interpreted, acted on, and affirmed in worship are all essential for the "traditioning" and "transforming" goals of Christian education to be realized. The configuration and intersection of congregational functions offer a matrix within which education "happens." Education as a discrete activity may center more on one activity than on another, but it is not possible without the carrying out of other functions.

A theological endorsement for such a position comes from Bernard Cooke's first "basic understanding," that on the church. One reason the church is called to clarity about its self-understanding is that its life is the locale of what people *really* come to believe about Christianity. The church is not "that through which Christians pass in order to reach God." The church is *themselves*, the body of Christ, "the context of the divine presence." To understand and to *be* the church is of critical importance, Cooke says, because "the experience of being part of a Christian congregation has informally imparted the awareness of Christianity that is basically operative in most people's faith."[33] Formulated understanding helps the church to be what it says it is. It is there, in the congregation, where symbols are encountered, with the added depth of shared meanings in the community of faith.[34]

What we have said points to what might well be called the "genius" of congregational education. At the same time that we affirm the validity of the term, let us consider one additional comment. If the potential "genius" is to be realized, then pain, conflict, and struggle are involved. Digging into the context and fuller interpretation of any of the immediately preceding comments would confirm this statement. More explicitly, note that The Church of the Covenant (see the companion volume, *Tensions Between Citizenship and Discipleship: A Case Study*, and references throughout this volume) experienced conflict within families as well as among members.[35] Outside influences were sometimes more powerful than those within the congregation. Studying the Bible did not always produce a clear mandate for action. But the education was real, though costly; it involved decisions of significance and worship that affirmed God's presence and care.

Or again, in connection with the same point, consider Brueggemann's reflections on the conversation "at the wall." One test of the conversation "behind the wall" (for our purposes here, most nearly related to what we are calling congregational education) comes at the point of its power to challenge "the dominant rationality" at the same time that it holds out hope for "a genuinely new thing" and is itself critiqued by that which stands over against it.[36] We have only begun to explore the implications for congregational education growing out of Brueggemann's textual study.

Even granted these reminders, even granted that congregational education must become bilingual, we affirm the conclusion that, for this moment, the setting of the congregation is basic for education. But just when congregational education seems to present itself as the working arena for building into the future, there may be other forms embryonic in the goals and strategies agreed upon here. Such a movement from stability to change has always characterized education. But for the present, all we can do is to act on what we see. The vision held by this particular band of disciples, called Christians, is yet to be worked out with disciplined devotion if the education is indeed to be "for the future good of the world."

In Conclusion

Looking back on the experience of thinking and being together, members of the Seminar might note, if questioned, that they have not only thought *about* education, they have also *been educated*—a kind of model of theological education for the future, both in graduate theological schools (especially) and in congregations. But questions move with us into the future. As we assert the potential of congregational education, we must ask: How do we relate the congregation to other institutions and agencies in a kind of ecology of education that opens new horizons and new possibilities? Another question. Horace Bushnell, mentioned above, firmly believed that the organic unity of the family made it the prime setting for Christian nurture. For him, parental nurture of their children was indeed a "training into Christ. . . . That training will secure the real initiation of their children into a state of genuine discipleship."[37] So *that* is the way discipleship comes into being! But Bushnell lived in the nineteenth century, not in the twentieth. What he feared—a replacement of the family responsibilities by the growing Sunday school movement—is now nearer reality. What *is* the appropriate and realistic relationship between congregational education and family nurture? Finally, perhaps most difficult of all, what do we do, in addition to thinking clearly, about education for both discipleship and citizenship? One thing, of course, is to work back through these essays with an eye to answering that question. Another is to invite a growing circle of Christians concerned for the future to work together in "doing" the answer.

Kierkegaard's *Concluding Unscientific Postscript* was a great volume, larger than the *Philosophical Fragments* to which it was a postscript. But H. Richard Niebuhr's concluding postscript, the last chapter in his *Christ and Culture,* ended in a statement that, strangely enough, is an appropriate ending for this volume.

> To make our decisions in faith is to make them in view of the fact that no single man [or woman] or group or historical time is the church; but that there is a church of faith in which we do our partial, relative work and on which we count. It is to make them in view of the fact that Christ is risen from the dead, and is not only the head of the church but the redeemer of the world. It is to make them in view of the fact that the world of culture—man's [and woman's] achievement—exists within the world of grace—God's Kingdom.[38]

NOTES

1. It is interesting to note that H. Richard Niebuhr in his *Christ and Culture* (New York: Harper & Brothers, 1951) called his concluding chapter "A Concluding Unscientific Postscript." What Niebuhr did was

to offer his reflection on what he had just presented as alternatives to the relationship between Christ and culture, noting the tentative nature of his analysis and raising more questions for future consideration. In that sense, the chapter here is more Niebuhrian than Kierkegaardian.

2. See, in this volume, Mary C. Boys, "Religious Education: A Map of the Field," p. 125.

3. See, in this volume, e.g., Don S. Browning, "Religious Education as Growth in Practical Theological Reflection and Action," especially his analysis of the aretaic perspectives on the five dimensions of practical moral thinking (pp. 154–60). He sees in the five types of developmental theory a "characterological counterpart" to the five dimensions of the objective or "principled side" of practical moral reason. His analysis is helpful.

4. Note the way in which foundational questions basic to all approaches are related to the classic expressions which appear at the "intersection of a particular theological perspective with a particular educational outlook" (Boys, "Religious Education," p. 105). Different ways of interpreting would be necessary for each expression. For example, *doctrine* would likely be a beginning point for the expression called "evangelism." On the other hand, the formulation of the meaning of experience by *naming* that experience would be an interpretative activity *leading* to doctrine, an approach more consistent with the "religious education" expression. Implications from other expressions could be drawn. In fact, as hermeneutical issues were raised in the Seminar, discussion often pushed back to assumptions regarding the nature of education.

5. It is interesting to note that Browning sees the Christian educator as more concerned about the "characterological counterpart" in his five dimensions of practical moral thinking than about the "principled" levels of the reflection he describes (Browning, "Religious Education as Growth," p. 154). Is he making this judgment descriptively or normatively? Many educators may seem to rely more on Browning's "aretaic dimensions," but there are many others who find themselves more at home with his "objective" categories. Boys's categories of "classic expressions" would certainly allow for differing emphases.

6. See, in this volume, Bernard Cooke, "Basic Christian Understandings," p. 81. Emphasis added.

7. James T. Borhek and Richard F. Curtis, *A Sociology of Belief* (New York: John Wiley & Sons, 1975), p. 23.

8. See Boys's interpretation of her own position, pp. 124–25. She advocates "dialogical education," respect for the individual conscience, and making traditions "accessible" through education, not imposing them.

9. Browning, "Religious Education as Growth," p. 134.

10. Ibid., p. 154.

11. See, in this volume, Walter Brueggemann, "The Legitimacy of a Sectarian Hermeneutic: 2 Kings 18—19," pp. 28–29.

12. Members of the Seminar, when they spent time together in presenting their own "social location" and its resultant formative influences on their lives, experienced the truth of this statement for themselves. Mary Boys's exposition of her own perspective is instructive at this point. See pp. 99–100 in her essay in this volume.

13. The Church of the Covenant's leaders who were involved in the sanctuary decision met with members of the Seminar in October 1984 at Christian Theological Seminary in Indianapolis. See Nelle G. Slater, ed., *Tensions Between Citizenship and Discipleship: A Case Study* (New York: Pilgrim Press, 1989).

14. George Albert Coe, *What Is Christian Education?* (New York: Charles Scribner's Sons, 1929), p. 29. Coe did not deny the value of tradition in determining the shape of the new world. His view of education simply necessitated engagement with social concerns.

15. See Horace Bushnell, *Christian Nurture* (New Haven: Yale University Press, 1947). The first two chapters were published in 1846, the others added in 1861. One of the major influences in religious education in the United States, Bushnell lamented the rampant individualism he saw in revivalism and elsewhere. For him, there was an organic unity in the family, manifest in the sacrament of baptism, that pointed to the day-by-day activities and conversations of the family as the natural learning environment for the child. Even physical nurture, for him, was a "means of grace." Thus there were "evil results of the wrong feeding of children" (see Part III of this volume).

16. Boys, "Religious Education," p. 124.

17. See, in this volume, Karen Lebacqz, "Pain and Pedagogy: A Modest Proposal," p. 164.

18. Boys, "Religious Education," p. 124.

19. Cooke, "Basic Christian Understandings," p. 79.

20. Ibid., p. 80.

21. Ibid., pp. 80–81.

22. See, in this volume, John Coleman, "The Two Pedagogies: Discipleship and Citizenship," p. 51.

23. See the analysis and conclusions of Boys, "Religious Education," pp. 122–23.

24. Coleman, "The Two Pedagogies," pp. 69–72.

25. Ibid., p. 72.

26. Quoted from Thomas Green's manuscript "Walls: Education in Communities of Text and Liturgy." Such an understanding was assumed by Seminar members.

27. Boys, "Religious Education," pp. 124–25.

28. Brueggemann, "The Legitimacy of a Sectarian Hermeneutic," p. 7.

29. Cooke, "Basic Christian Understandings," p. 95.

30. One example comes from Professor Richard Osmer, of Union Theological Seminary in Virginia. His 1986 fall-term course, "Theological Reflection in the Local Congregation," utilizes Browning's "objective" five dimensions in a disciplined way to reflect theologically on case studies by upper-level students returning from the intern year or summer field education. Response verifies the usefulness of the categories, Osmer says.

31. Hans-Ruedi Weber, *Experiments with Bible Study* (Geneva: World Council of Churches, 1981), p. vii.

32. See Carl S. Dudley, ed., *Building Effective Ministry: Theory and Practice in the Local Church* (San Francisco: Harper & Row, 1983); see also the extensive bibliography on congregational education, pp. 246–56. Note especially Denham Grierson, *Transforming a People of God* (Melbourne, Australia: Joint Board of Christian Education of Australia and New Zealand, 1984). It has to do with congregational education and is especially helpful at the point of analyzing the symbols and rituals that give meaning to the life of a "faith community."

33. See Cooke, "Basic Christian Understandings," p. 81.

34. A letter from Nelle Slater, Seminar member, undated, makes this point, and adds: "The inner relationship between a believer and the symbols of faith, not their meaning, but their meaningfulness to the believer, is given added depth in a community of commitment. There one's faith may be experienced."

35. See especially C. Ellis Nelson's article, "Some Educational Aspects of Conflict," in Slater, *Tensions Between Citizenship and Discipleship.*

36. See Brueggemann, "The Legitimacy of a Sectarian Hermeneutic," pp. 17–23.

37. Bushnell, *Christian Nurture,* p. 94. See also Nelson, "Some Educational Aspects of Conflict," in Slater, *Tensions Between Citizenship and Discipleship.*

38. Niebuhr, *Christ and Culture,* p. 256.